BATSFORD'S CHESS BIBLE

BATSFORD'S
CHESS
BIBLE

From beginner to winner with moves, techniques and strategies

Sean Marsh

BATSFORD

Dedicated to my parents, brothers and sisters, JH, CL, GSM and to the memories of Bob Wade and Mike Closs.

First published in the United Kingdom in 2014 by B.T. Batsford
43 Great Ormond Street
London WC1N 3HZ

An imprint of B.T. Batsford Holdings Ltd

ISBN: 9781849947091

A CIP catalogue record for this book is available from the British Library.

10 9 8 7 6 5 4 3 2

Repro by Dot Gradations Ltd, UK
Printed and bound by Toppan Leefung Ltd, China

This book can be ordered direct from the publisher at www.batsfordbooks.com, or try your local bookshop.

p178 photograph © Mary Evans Picture Library.
All other photographs © Alamy.

CONTENTS

REMEMBERING BOB WADE

International Master Robert G. Wade OBE (1921-2008) wrote a best-selling chess book for Batsford which was first published in 1974, called *Playing Chess*. Revised editions, with a new title, appeared in 1984 and 1991. It was a very popular book which appealed to novices and more experienced players alike. This book is modelled on Bob Wade's book and is aimed at a similar readership, offering a sweeping coverage of chess and chess players, from learning the moves to appreciating the games of the World Champions.

Bob was a strong player, winning the championships of New Zealand three times (1944, 1945 and 1948) and Great Britain (1952 and 1970). He earned the title of International Master in 1958 and represented both New Zealand and England at international level. He was an excellent author but better known for his key editorial role in making B.T. Batsford the world's top chess publisher in the late 1960s and 1970s. In this capacity, his great knowledge and experience was supported by his huge library of chess books and magazines.

Moreover, he generously gave his time to tutor and advise a countless number of chess players, both young and old, and even helped the legendary Bobby Fischer to prepare for his titanic World Championship match against Boris Spassky in 1972. In 1979 he was awarded the OBE for his enormous contributions to British chess.

When Bob died there was no shortage of glowing tributes from players of all ages and levels of chess ability, from top Grandmasters to parents of junior players. I would now like to share some memories of my own meetings with Bob.

We first met in 1988, at the very start of my career in teaching chess in schools. Bob came to Teesside to deliver a coaching course and I spent as much time as possible grilling him about his experiences with Viktor Korchnoi, Bobby Fischer and other giants of the chess world. He was very willing to share his stories but there was a certain reluctance to go into detail about his dealings with Fischer. Bob expressed great praise for my coaching skills, telling me I would "easily go on to become a top national coach." Needless to say, such words of encouragement served as a big confidence booster to me and sum up how inspirational and generous Bob could be.

We met again at the press conference for the 1989 London Candidates Matches (eliminators for the World Championship) featuring Jonathan Speelman vs. Jan Timman and Anatoly Karpov vs. Artur Yusupov. Clearly sensing I was a little overawed at being in such exalted company, Bob made a point of introducing me to as many famous Grandmasters as possible. Afterwards he took me on a mini-tour of chess-related London locations, including various specialist book shops and the Batsford offices. Intrigued by the extent of his famous collection of chess literature,

I asked him how many chess books he actually owned and he said he had no idea at all and that counting them would be a retrograde step anyway. He came out of one bookshop with a couple of volumes on 'Go' and mentioned in passing that his collection of books on that game was very large too.

As we walked the streets of London, I quizzed him further about his contact with Fischer. He was undoubtedly still in touch with the 11th World Champion but had to be a little careful how much he said. He did tell me that when Fischer needed him, contact was made "in a roundabout sort of way" and that there had been plans for Fischer and Spassky to play a match in South Africa, an unexpected choice of venue. However, the plans had fallen through (this was still three years before Fischer emerged from his chess exile to play the 1992 'World Championship' rematch).

We met a few more times after that, always in London. I remember travelling by tube with him on the way back from one of the Kasparov vs. Kramnik World Championship match games in 2000. He pulled some chess magazines from the pockets of his coat and showed me some striking examples of three-piece attacks, which he said juniors found particularly difficult to carry out in their own games.

Our final encounter was at the 2008 Staunton Memorial tournament. Not surprisingly, at 87(!) years of age, he was very tired after one of his losses and I'm not sure he even recognised me at first. Nevertheless, he recovered his spirits quickly and we chatted about his experiences of playing against far younger players.

I had written to him shortly before his death to invite him to take part in my series of interviews for CHESS Magazine. I was confidently awaiting a positive response when the news of his death suddenly appeared online.

At the next Staunton Memorial tournament, in 2009, I was present at the Bob Wade Memorial Evening, which featured a witty, moving and memorable tribute by none other than Viktor Korchnoi. The remarkable array of chess players present on that evening, including numerous Grandmasters, further emphasized how much of an influence Bob had on the growth of British chess and how much appreciation there was for his unstinting services to the great game.

I sincerely hope that *Batsford's Chess Bible*, which was inspired by Bob Wade's original book, will help aspiring chess players improve their skills and enhance their appreciation of the great game. I hope also that Bob, wherever he may be, will approve of my attempt to keep the spirit of his fine work alive.

Sean Marsh
January 2014

INTRODUCTION

Chess is an easy game to learn but a difficult one to master. Virtually anyone in the world can learn the basic moves in a matter of minutes and, unlike the majority of sports and games, it provides the opportunity for juniors to battle on equal terms with adults. It is a universal game that can be played anywhere at any time – even on a small travel set or a mobile phone. Millions of people play chess via the Internet every day, against opponents from all over the world, and it doesn't require a stadium or football pitch, just an 8x8 checkered board and 32 chess pieces.

THIS BOOK HAS SEVERAL AIMS

1) Using our quick start guides, to teach novices of all ages the basics - so they can begin to play chess in the shortest possible time.

2) After a little practice, to encourage new players to return to the book and move on to more challenging work, such as the study of tactics, positional play and the principles of chess openings.

3) To introduce a number of chess heroes and examples of their skilful play. Hopefully, these instructive games will whet the appetites of readers, who will then be inspired to look at other masterpieces and develop a lasting interest in the history and culture of chess.

4) To encourage independent work by means of test yourself puzzles. So turn the page and step inside the wonderful world of chess...

THE BASICS

Chess Notation

A permanent record of chess moves can be made either on a hard copy scoresheet or a computer database. This enables you to replay your own games as well as those of Grandmasters and World Champions, past and present, from which you can learn the art of tactics and strategy.

We use the coordinates of the chess board to record the moves and thereby document games for future reference. The method is exactly the same as for the game of Battleships and for reading maps. Each piece on the board is represented by a letter, apart from the pawns which don't need one.

K for king
Q for queen
R for rook
B for bishop
N for knight (to avoid confusion with K for king)

Various symbols are used for special moves.
O-O for castling on the kingside.
O-O-O for castling on the queenside.
A capture is indicated by '**x**' A check is indicated by '**+**'.
! means 'good move'.
!! means 'exceptional move'.
? means 'bad move'.
?? means 'blunder' (a very bad move indeed).
!? means 'interesting move', which may turn out to be good.
?! means 'dubious move', which may turn out to be bad.

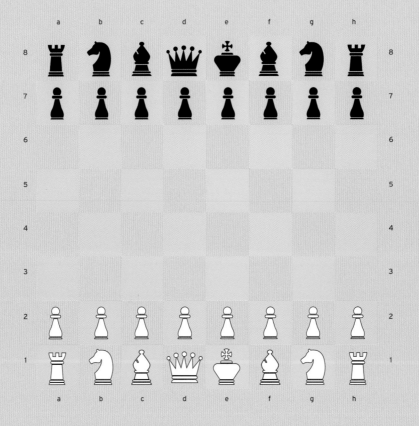

PIECES AND MOVES

♟ The Pawn

Pawns move one square forward (or, optionally, two on their very first move only). They capture one square diagonally forward. On reaching the end of the board, they are exchanged for another piece of the same colour, i.e. a queen, rook, knight or bishop – but never a king. This is known as 'pawn promotion'.

The Pawn in Detail

The pawn is the lowest value unit in a game of chess. The name is derived from peón, the Spanish word for foot-soldier. The normal move of a pawn is one square forward. But, when moving for the very first time in the game, it also has the option of advancing two squares.

Pawns capture enemy pieces by moving one square diagonally forward. Think of a foot-soldier, marching into battle against an enemy foot-soldier. They both have shields to protect themselves from frontal blows, so they have to 'stab' each other at an oblique angle.

Pawns can never retreat or move sideways. They cannot move diagonally unless they are capturing an opponent's pawn or piece.

Both players start the game with eight pawns. Generally speaking, they are at their strongest when they can protect each other and at their weakest when they are isolated.

♝ The Bishop

Bishops move as far as they want along an unobstructed diagonal line. They cannot jump over other pieces or change direction in the process of making a move.

The Bishop in Detail

In days of old, the role of the bishop was taken by an 'elephant.' But, as this animal was unfamiliar to European eyes, and the role of the clergy was pronounced, the chess piece became the bishop as we know it today. The design of this chess piece is in the form of a mitre – the ceremonial headdress of real-life bishops.

Since bishops can only ever move on diagonal lines, they can never change the colour of the squares on which they operate. Therefore each bishop can only ever visit half of the squares on a chess board. Bishops are long range pieces and work best as a pair, since then they cover all 64 squares of the chess board.

Both players start the game with two bishops; one on the white squares and one on the black squares.

♜ The Rook

Rooks move as far they want along unobstructed straight lines.

The Rook in Detail

The word 'rook' is derived from rukh, an Old Persian word for chariot, which was the original name for this piece. However, today, novices often refer to rooks as 'castles' due to their turreted appearance. Castles were a very familiar sight to Europeans in the Middle Ages, so the physical appearance of the piece was changed.

Rooks are powerful, long-range pieces. Both players have two rooks and these are placed in the corners of the board at the start of play.

♞ The Knight

A knight moves one square in a straight line, in any direction, and then two squares to the side. Or, alternatively, two squares in a straight line, in any direction, and then one square to the side. It is the only piece that can jump over other pieces and pawns.

The Knight in Detail

Knights represent cavalry or horsemen. Novices will habitually call them 'horses' (or even 'ponies' and 'donkeys').

The move of the knight is the trickiest for novices to grasp and is best remembered by its 'L' shape. Every time it moves, it changes the colour of its square, hopping from white to black and then black to white.

Knights are allowed to jump over other pieces and pawns, regardless of whether or not they belong to the opponent's army or their own. Every other piece needs to wait until a pawn moves before it can be developed, but a knight can enter the game on the very first move.

They are short-range pieces and can only cover long distances in a slow and clumsy manner. However, they can cover every square of the board (which the long-range bishop cannot).

Each player starts the game with two knights.

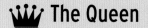 The Queen

The queen moves as far as she wants in any direction along unobstructed straight or diagonal lines.

The Queen in Detail

The queen is the most powerful chess piece, but this wasn't always the case. Until the 15th century the equivalent piece was called the fers, meaning a prime minister or counsellor and it could only move one square diagonally in any direction. Thus it was far from being a powerful piece.

It is not entirely clear why the rules were changed to allow the creation of a powerful female figure but in some parts of the world it remained a controversial decision for some time.

Given the power of the queen, it is very tempting for inexperienced players to bring her out into the game as soon as possible. Indeed, many games between novices are decided quickly by one side's queen racing into the action and either slaughtering the opponent's forces or delivering a very quick checkmate. Against more experienced players, however, this usually proves far too risky and leads to a serious loss of time or even the loss of the queen.

Each player starts with just one queen but pawns can promote to new queens, even if the original one is still on the board. It is technically possible – but very unlikely – for a player to end up with nine queens on the board at the same time.

Be careful with your queen!

♚ The King

Kings can only move one square at a time in any direction. They are special in that they cannot be captured.

The King in Detail

The king is the most important of all chess pieces, despite his very limited range of movement.

If a king is under attack from an enemy unit, it is said to be in 'check'. The king cannot be captured under any circumstances, so he has to try to escape from check immediately. If he cannot escape from check then he is in 'checkmate' and the opponent has won the game.

There are three ways to get out of check.

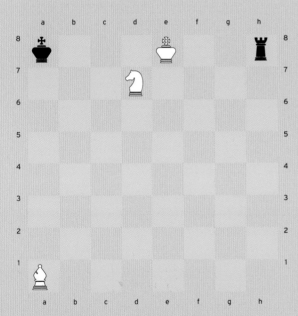

White to play and escape from check

The black rook is attacking the white king, so the king is in check. The three ways of getting out of check are:

1) Moving the king out of range of the checking piece. In this example, White can move his king to either f7 or e7.

2) Blocking the check. White can move his knight to f8, blocking the attack from the rook.

3) Taking the attacking piece. White's bishop can swoop down the long diagonal and capture the attacking rook.

If none of the three ways of escaping from check are possible then it is checkmate and the game ends.

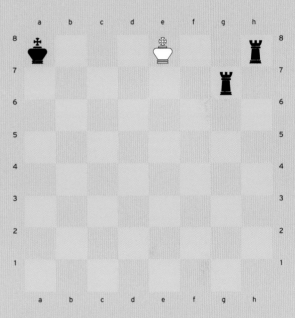

White to play

White cannot capture the attacking rook and has no way of blocking the check. His king cannot move to d7, e7 or f7 because the other rook is attacking those squares and a king is never allowed to move into a check. The white king has been checkmated and Black wins the game.

SPECIAL MOVES

In addition to the basic moves of the pieces, there are three special moves.

Pawn Promotion

Pawns gain in strength towards the end of the game. There is more chance of them reaching the other end of the board if there are fewer enemy pieces in the vicinity. Pawn promotion can be a winning strategy.

White to play

The material is equal in this position, but White's a-pawn can easily march to the end of the board without being stopped. From the diagram, play could continue: 1 a7 Kd7 2 a8=Q, leading to the next diagram.

Both sides still have an equal number of pieces, but White is winning easily. The queen is worth so much more than a pawn.

There are two common misconceptions about pawn promotions. Some novices think:

1) That a pawn must promote to a queen. Not true. You can promote a pawn to a queen, rook, bishop or knight. Ordinarily, of course, a queen is preferable to anything else. In fact, promotion to a rook, bishop or knight is called underpromotion.
2) That a pawn can only be promoted to a queen if the original queen has been captured and removed from the board. Again not true! A player can end up with several queens on the board. The next position is taken from a famous game between two of the world's strongest players.

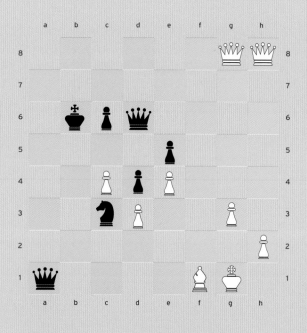

Bobby Fischer vs. Tigran Petrosian
Candidates Tournament, Yugoslavia, 1959

Both players have recently promoted one of their pawns and obtained new queens. The game eventually ended in a draw.

In the vast majority of games, a pawn promotion will result in a new queen appearing on the board. However, there are rare exceptions that may require promotion to another piece instead of a queen.

White to play

In this position, the most obvious move for White is to play 1 f8=Q. Unfortunately, Black would then win the game by playing 1 ...d1=Q checkmate. So White needs to realize that being first to promote to a queen isn't enough in this position. This should then lead to the discovery of the best move - underpromotion to a knight: 1 f8=N checkmate.

Checkmate

Castling

Castling is a special move involving a king and a rook.

White to play

White can castle in two different ways in this position. To castle on the kingside of the board (also known as 'castling short'), the king moves from e1 to g1 and the rook moves from h1 to f1, classed as all part of one and the same move.

White has castled on the kingside

To castle on the queenside of the board ('castling long') the king moves from e1 to c1 and the rook moves from a1 to d1, all in a single move.

White has castled on the queenside

The point of castling is to provide protection for the king and, at the same time, to bring the rook into play. Ordinarily, there will be pawns in front of the castled king, and usually a knight as well, to help with the defence.

The white king is very safe

It is advisable to castle as soon as possible. Novices are sometimes reluctant to place their king in the corner of the board, fearing it will present an easier target. That is not true. If one player castles and the other doesn't, it will be the side with the uncastled king who will more often find himself in trouble. Every good chess player will try to castle at the earliest opportunity.

Sometimes it is not possible to castle.

1) If the king has already moved, a player cannot castle.

2) If the rook has already moved, a player cannot castle. It will still be possible to castle on the opposite side of the board if the other rook has not yet moved.

3) If the king is in check, then castling is not allowed. If the check can be met without having to move the king, then castling will still be possible later on.

4) If there is anything blocking the path between the king and the rook, then castling is not allowed.

White to play

In this position, White cannot castle on the kingside until he develops the knight and bishop, but he is allowed to castle on the queenside.

5) A player is not allowed to castle if, in the process, the king would have travel through a square which would subject the king to a check.

White to play

Here, White cannot castle on the kingside because both the f1 and g1 squares are under attack by enemy pieces. He can castle on the queenside instead, even though the a1 square is attacked by the bishop, as the king will not have to cross that square.

The En Passant Pawn Capture

This special move is tricky and one that novices often initially struggle to understand.

Originally, pawns could only advance one square at a time. The rules changed in the 1400s to allow the pawns a choice of advancing either one or two squares on their first move, as is the case today. This led to a new option for playing with the pawns.

White to play

It seemed a little cheeky to be able to take advantage of the new rule in this way, so another new rule was introduced – the *en passant* capture. This rule allows the white pawn to capture the black pawn as if it had just moved a single square.

Black to play

Black has a winning advantage in this position. Using the old rules, the only possible move for his g-pawn would be to g6, whereupon White would be able to capture it with his own pawn by moving one square diagonally forward. Under the new rules, Black could push the g-pawn two squares forward to the g5 square, and thus evade capture.

Black to play

White has just captured the black pawn *en passant*. The phrase means 'in passing', which is a good description of the action of the white pawn. The *en passant* capture has to be made immediately. If White delays, he forfeits the right to make this special capture. In the position given above, White has emerged with a winning position as Black's knight is too clumsily placed to prevent the promotion of the g-pawn.

Only pawns can capture *en passant* and they can only capture other pawns with this move.

THE VALUES OF THE PIECES

It is interesting to compare the qualities of the different pieces. It is essential to understand their respective values, otherwise you won't know what is a good exchange and what would be a bad mistake.

Kings cannot be awarded a value as they can never be exchanged. In simple terms, the other pieces are worth:
Pawn = 1 point
Knight = 3 points
Bishop = 3 points
Rook = 5 points
Queen = 9 points

Clearly, under normal circumstances, it would be a bad mistake to swap a queen for a lower value piece.

1 Qxd8+ is just a blunder here. Black will simply recapture with 1...Rxd8 with a winning advantage. The queen is worth much more than a bishop. However, there are sometimes other factors which would reduce the nominal values of the pieces to secondary importance.

White to play

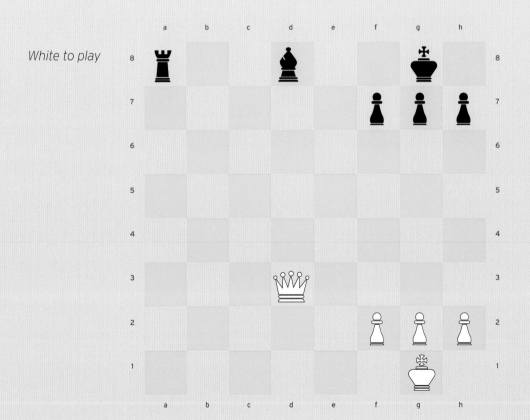

White to play

The addition of the white rook makes a big difference. White can play 1 Qxd8+ Rxd8 and 2 Rxd8 checkmate. Even though the queen is worth three times as much as the bishop, the values of the pieces are no longer the most important factor. Checkmate ends the game.

With knights and bishops each worth three points, it can be a very difficult task to evaluate whether or not it is a good idea to exchange one for the other. Indeed, even strong players can struggle with such a decision. Comparing the activity of each piece makes the task easier.

White to play

White could exchange his knight for the black bishop by 1 Nxd7 Kxd7. However, the bishop is blocked in by its own pawns and is struggling to make any impact on the game. The knight is in an excellent position and has a much greater chance of making a significant impact on the game. So, in this particular case, White should keep the knight on the board and decline to exchange.

White to play

This time the bishop enjoys much more freedom than in the previous example. White can happily exchange with 1 Nxe7 Kxe7.

Bishops prefer open positions, where they are not blocked in by lots of pawns. Knights prefer closed positions in which they can hop in and out of the pawns.

WINNING, DRAWING AND LOSING

A game of chess has three possible results for a player: win, draw or loss.

Three Ways to Lose
You will lose a game of chess if:

1) Your king is checkmated

2) You resign the game (if you have a serious material deficit or believe checkmate is inevitable)

3) You are using a chess clock and you run out of time.

Losing at Chess
The aim of the game of chess is to checkmate the opponent's king. It sounds so simple: after all, the king, despite being the most important piece on the board, can only move one square at a time and requires protection from his army. Indeed, achieving checkmate against a novice can be very easy and it often goes like this:

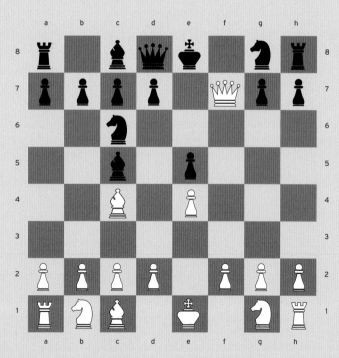

1 e4 e5
2 Bc4 Nc6
3 Qf3 (or 3 Qh5) Bc5
4 Qxf7 checkmate.

This checkmate is so common that it even has a name: Scholar's Mate or Schoolboy's Mate. If the opponent plays very weakly, right from the start, an even faster checkmate is possible.

1 g4 e5

2 f3 Qh4 checkmate.

Though this is rather insultingly known as Fool's Mate, the best way to remember such checkmates is to fall for them – and then it is unlikely you will allow a repeat performance. To prevent Fool's Mate, it is enough to know that moving pawns on the kingside so early in the game leads to potentially serious weaknesses. Numerous disasters can occur on the h4-e1 diagonal for White, and along the corresponding h5-e8 diagonal for Black.

There are several ways to guard against Scholar's Mate. Logically, the queen can only get to the magic f7 square if she is allowed to do so. Black needs to be aware that as soon as the queen comes into play, she will be hoping to land the knockout blow. But it is easy to block her path.

1 e4 e5

2 Qf3 Nf6

That's all there is to it. If White continues with 3 Bc4, Black doesn't have to worry, since, as long as the knight remains on f6, the queen won't be able to deliver the checkmate. Indeed, after 3 ...Bc5 Black can quickly castle (4 ...0-0) and he already has the better position. On f3, the white queen not only blocks the best square for her own knight, but may even find herself being chased around the board just to evade capture, particularly after Black develops the queen's knight (...Nc6, with the idea of ...Nd4, attacking the queen).

White could try an alternative route to Scholar's Mate, but with care and attention Black will have no problems.

1 e4 e5
2 Qh5

Black must avoid the blunder 2 ...g6?? which allows 3 Qxe5+ and 4 Qxh8 – a good example of a *fork*, to which we will return in the section on *Tactical Weapons*. It is important to protect the e5 pawn and this is easily achieved with a developing move.

2 ...Nc6
3 Bc4 g6

Now 3 ...g6 is fine as 4 Qxe5+?? doesn't work (because of 4 ...Nxe5) and there is no way for the queen to reach f7 and deliver checkmate. White can renew the threat by retreating with his queen.

4 Qf3

We now know that Black can easily block this attempt.

4 ...Nf6

Black should be very happy with this position. He will soon castle (after 5 ...Bg7, to plug the holes in his defence) and then think about chasing the white queen around.

Once a player has learned to avoid such early catastrophes, the games will go on longer and become more difficult. Naturally, every threat to the king must be taken extremely seriously. There is little point being massively ahead in material if a player is going to lose concentration and allow the opponent to deliver a one-move checkmate. A momentary lapse of concentration in most other sports or games doesn't always deny players ultimate victory. For example, a football team leading 5-0 could lose their focus for a minute and carelessly allow a goal to go in at the other end. It's annoying, but ultimately the final score of 5-1 isn't all that different from 5-0. In chess it is different and one little slip can easily cost the whole game, thus ruining several hours of hard work.

It makes perfect to sense to familiarize oneself with as many of the standard checkmate patterns as possible. Here are a few essentials which will crop up time and again.

Checkmating with Queens

The queen is such a powerful piece as she can control many squares at the same time. She doesn't need much help to force a checkmate. The next three positions show common ways to finish off a game.

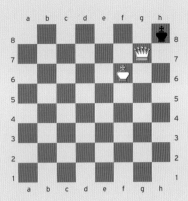

The only way to master these basic checkmates is to practice until one's technique is perfect. Simply get together with a friend and set up this position.

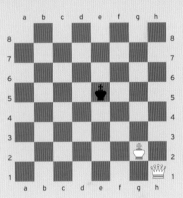

White to play

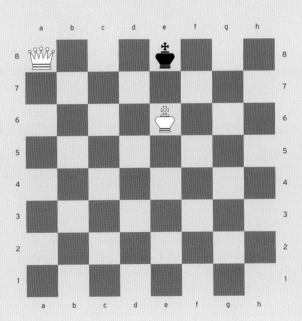

Note that the white pieces are in poor positions on the side of the board, with the king blocking some of the queen's power. The black king stands proudly in the centre. Take turns with your friend, with one of you handling the white pieces first. Try to force the black king to the edge of the board in order to reach one of the checkmate positions given above. The white queen needs help from her king; they must work as a team. Black's king must stay in the centre of the board for as long as possible and move away only if he is forced to do so.

White can start to force the king out of the centre once this position has been achieved.

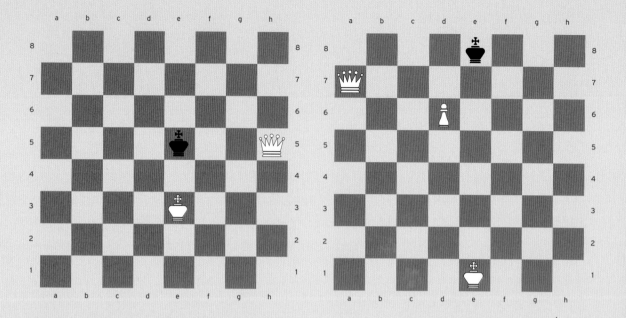

White's queen could be on h5, g5, c5, b5 or a5 and the effect will be the same. If the queen stands on d5 or f5 then Black would simply capture it and the game would end in an instant draw. The most important feature of the position is the way the kings are facing each other.

The white king stops the black one from advancing (because the squares d4, e4 and f4 are checked by the white king). So Black has to step back, where he is closer to the edge of the board. White will continue to force the king back using this pattern until Black cannot run any further and then it will be checkmate.

Queen checkmates don't always require the help of the king. The queen just needs to be protected by something else, even if it is just a little pawn.

Here White will play **1 Qe7** checkmate. 1 ...Kxe7 is an illegal move because the pawn is protecting e7 and kings cannot place themselves in check. Every other piece can help the queen too.

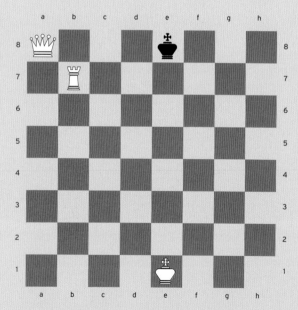

This is another very common pattern. The white rook stops the king from leaving the back row and the queen delivers the checkmate.

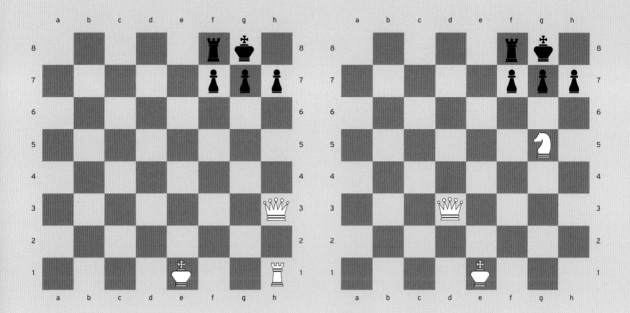

Lining up a queen and a rook on the same file creates a very powerful attacking unit. White plays **1 Qxh7** and it is checkmate. Black cannot reply with 1 ...Kxh7 because the rook is protecting the queen.

allows White to play 1 Qxh7 checkmate.

Sometimes the queen doesn't need any help from her own pieces.

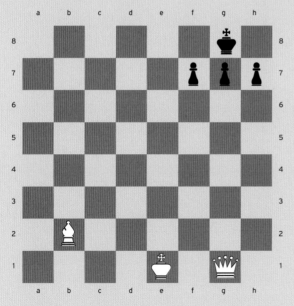

The bishop and the queen are both aiming at g7. White plays 1 Qxg7 checkmate.

The knight attacks the h7 square and this

1 Qa8 is checkmate. Note how the black king is trapped helplessly behind his own pawns. This is called a back row checkmate (or back rank checkmate) and is very common.

Checkmating with Rooks

This is the standard checkmate pattern for a king and rook. It is absolutely essential to practice this way of finishing a game as it will happen very often. Practice with a friend from this position.

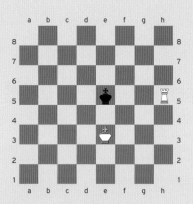

Black to play

The black king is forced to leave the centre and White will repeat this pattern until he is forced to the edge of the board and checkmated.

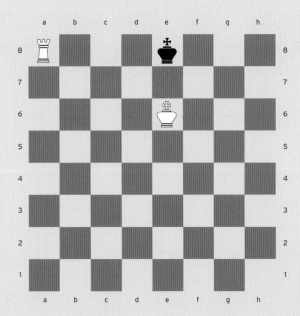

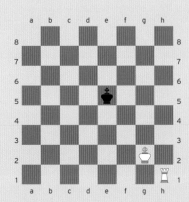

White to play

The technique of forcing the black king from the centre is identical to the one we used for the queen checkmates.

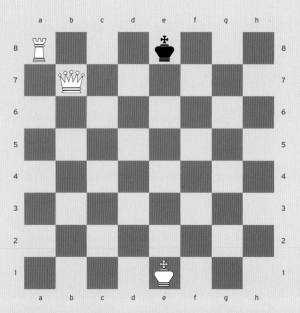

This is very similar to one of the earlier queen checkmates. This time the queen prevents the black king from escaping and the rook delivers the checkmate.

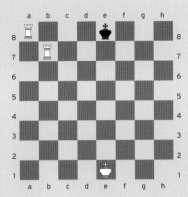

The same pattern with two rooks. The rook, currently on a8, could just as well be on b8, c8, g8 or h8 and it would still be checkmate. The rook on b7 could be on a7, c7, g7 or h7 and it would still prevent the king from escaping.

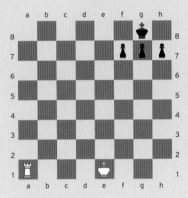

Just like the queen, rooks can produce a back row (or back rank) checkmate. Here, **1 Ra8** checkmate ends the game.

Rooks team up well with other pieces. Here, **1 Ra8** is checkmate, even though it looks as if Black can escape with 1 ...Kg7. The problem is the white bishop, attacking g7 and making 1...Kg7 an illegal move.

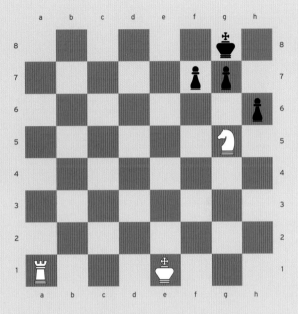

This time the knight attacks the potential escape square (or flight square). **1 Ra8** is checkmate.

A pair of rooks makes a strong team. Black's rook on a8 is protecting the back row, but this is not enough as it is outgunned. White will play **1 Rc8+** and when Black replies **1 ...Rxc8**, the second rook moves in for the kill with **2 Rxc8** checkmate.

Checkmating with Bishops

Bishops, knights and pawns don't checkmate as often as queens and rooks because they are not as powerful and usually require more assistance. It is still possible to checkmate the opponent very early on in the game with a single bishop, but only in response to some very weak moves. For example, after **1 f4 e6 2 b3 Be7 3 g4**, Black can win easily.

Black to play

3 ...Bh4 checkmate.

Bishops are stronger when they work in pairs, with one bishop controlling the black squares and the other controlling the white squares.

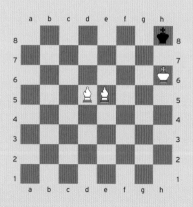

Checkmate, but note that the bishops still need the help of the king, despite the black king being in a very weak position on the side of the board.

Checkmating with Knights

Knights can do something no other piece can do: they can jump over other pieces and pawns. That makes it impossible to block a knight check and allows knights to create some unique checkmate patterns.

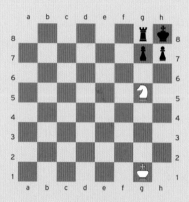

White can play **1 Nf7** checkmate. This sort of position - with the checkmated king being blocked in by his own pieces - is called a smothered mate. The most famous type of smothered mate involves a queen sacrifice and is known as Philidor's Legacy.

Jan Timman vs. Nigel Short
Tilburg, 1990
White to play

26 Qc4+ Kh8
27 Nf7+ Kg8
28 Nh6+ Kh8
Everything is ready for the queen sacrifice.

29 Qg8+ Rxg8
30 Nf7 checkmate **1-0**
A sequence well worth remembering.

Checkmating with Pawns

Pawns can checkmate kings but they have to be very close indeed to the enemy king and usually need a lot of help from other pieces. Nevertheless it can be done.

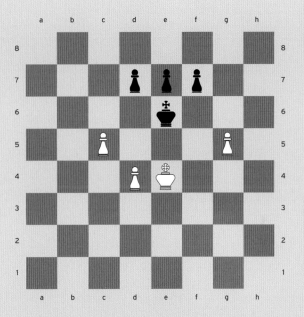

White can checkmate the black king with **1 d5** checkmate.

In addition to being checkmated, there are two other ways to lose a game of chess. The majority of games end with one player resigning. This is done by simply saying "I resign" or even by just turning down one's king. If using chess clocks, stopping the clocks from ticking is also a way of resigning.

Players only resign if their position is utterly hopeless and/or checkmate is inevitable. Novices and juniors are advised to play on, instead of resigning, no matter how bad the position. Another novice may not know how to finish off a game and could make lots of mistakes which would give the other player fresh chances. It is also instructive and useful for the novice to see how a player finishes off the game. Every checkmate pattern you can remember can be turned into a weapon to be used in future battles.

The third way to lose also involves chess clocks (which most novices and juniors won't need to use until they gain more experience). Clocks are set to allow a certain amount of time for each game and if one player runs out of time then he loses the game (or draws the game, if the opponent doesn't have enough material to force a checkmate).

Different Ways to Draw

Not every game of chess ends in a victory. Indeed, in games between Grandmasters, there will usually be more draws than wins. In the 1927 World Championship match between Capablanca and Alekhine there were 34 games and no fewer than 25 of them ended in draws. Alekhine won the match by six wins to three as draws did not count towards the final score. When Karpov and Kasparov started their first World Championship match in September 1984, they could hardly have predicted they would still be playing the same match in March 1985, having played 48 games and - incredibly - drawn 40 of them. Unprecedentedly, at this point the match was abandoned with Karpov leading the match with five wins to three.

There are numerous ways in which a game of chess can end in a draw.

Mutual Agreement

The simplest method - and by far the most common - is for one player to offer a draw and for the other player to accept. This is done by asking, "would you like a draw?" or by simply saying "draw?" The opponent will normally spend a little time thinking about it. The draw offer cannot be retracted but is no longer valid if the opponent makes another move on the board or verbally declines the offer. It is a good idea to ponder why someone has made a draw offer. Do they think they have the worse position and are they trying to salvage a draw from probable defeat? Is the position a dead draw anyway? Does the opponent (or his team) require half a point to clinch a match victory or first place in a tournament? It can sometimes be a tricky decision. Novices and juniors are strongly advised to play on instead of agreeing to a draw. Every game should be a learning experience and the longer the game goes on, the more there is to learn.

Stalemate

Stalemate occurs when one side has no legal moves but is not in check.

Black to play

This is a common example of a stalemate position. Black cannot move his king anywhere without placing himself into check (which is illegal). The result of the game is a draw.

Stalemates frequently occur in games featuring novices who have not yet learned how to finish off opponents with a checkmate. A very common error is for a winning side to get carried away and become excited by the possibility of gaining extra queens by means of pawn promotions. If there is too much firepower on the board then the risk of accidentally allowing a stalemate increases.

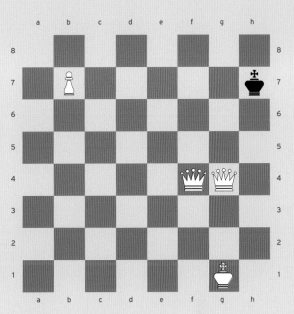

White to play

White could easily checkmate Black in one move with 1 Qh2. Getting another queen with 1 b8=Q is a big mistake, because it leaves Black without a legal move and the game ends in a draw by stalemate.

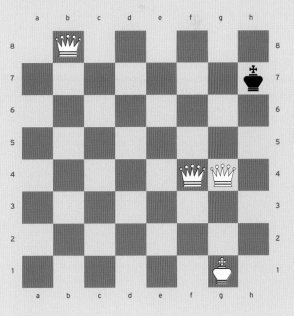

Stalemate!

Not all stalemates arise from careless blunders and sloppy technique. Some require inspiration and terrific imagination to work.

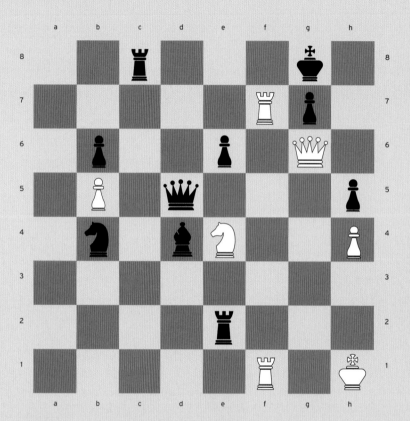

Tony Miles vs. Mikhail Nedobora
Seville, 1994
White to play

Tony Miles was one of England's greatest chess players. Indeed, he was the first English player to become a Grandmaster. He was noted as a tough battler who often found incredible resources in difficult positions.

This position looks dreadful for White. He is material down and his king is under heavy fire. Some players would resign here, but Miles found a way to force a draw.

41 Rf8+! Rxf8
42 Rxf8+ Kxf8

It looks even worse for Miles now, but he has spotted an excellent resource.

43 Qf7+!!
The game was agreed drawn here. Black's only possible move is to capture the queen with his king (43 ...Kxf7), leading to the next position.

White to play

It is not possible for White to move anything without placing himself in check, so the game ends in a draw by stalemate.

Perpetual Check

A perpetual check draws a game of chess by continually checking the enemy king (potentially forever) without being able to force a checkmate. The checked king cannot escape a perpetual check.

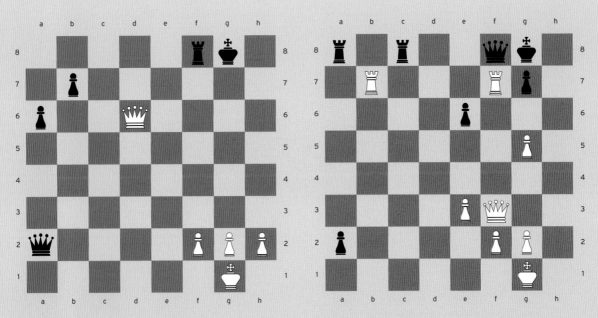

White to play

Black has a large material advantage and under normal circumstances he should win the game. Yet White can force a draw with a perpetual check. **1 Qg6+ Kh8 2 Qh6+ Kg8 3 Qg6+** and Black's king cannot escape the checks.

Perpetual check is often used to escape from a potentially losing position, even at the cost of a sacrifice.

Akiva Rubinstein vs. José Raul Capablanca
Berlin, 1928
White to play

This is a complicated position but Black seems to be on the point of winning. Rubinstein can capture the queen with 28 Rxf8+ but after 28 … Rxf8 his own queen is under attack and Black can promote his a-pawn to gain a new queen with his very next move (29 …a1=Q). Rubinstein escaped with **28 Rxg7+ Qxg7 29 Rxg7+ Kxg7 30 Qf6+ Kg8 31 Qg6+ Kf8 32 Qf6+** and the players agreed to a draw.

Repetition of Position

If the exact same position is repeated three times in a game of chess then it can end in a draw. It is not, however, an automatic draw; it is up to one of the players to claim the draw by pointing out to the opponent (or to the Arbiter - a type of chess referee - if one is present) that the same position is about to occur for the third time. The claim is usually made after writing down the next intended move on the scoresheet.

Boris Spassky vs.
Bobby Fischer
World Championship Match,
Reykjavik, 1972
White to play

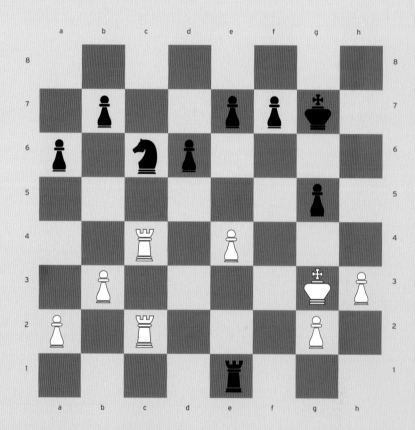

This position is from the 17th game of one of the most famous chess matches in history. Spassky has a slight material advantage (a rook for a knight and a pawn).

42 Rc1 Re2
43 R1c2 Re1
Reaching the position given in the diagram again.

44 Rc1 Re2
45 R1c2
At this point Fischer wrote down his next move - **45 ...Re1** - on his scoresheet (but didn't play the move on the board). He then informed the Arbiter that his intended move was going to bring about the same position for the third time. The Arbiter agreed and the game ended as a draw.

The game continues as normal if neither player claims a repetition, as in the next example.

John Van der Wiel vs. Anatoly Karpov
World Cup, Rotterdam, 1989

1 e4 e5	7 Bb3 d6
2 Nf3 Nc6	8 c3 0-0
3 Bb5 a6	9 h3 Re8
4 Ba4 Nf6	10 Ng5 Rf8
5 0-0 Be7	11 d4 Bb7
6 Re1 b5	12 Nf3 Re8

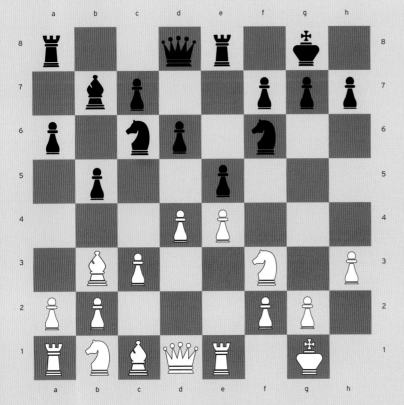

A standard position in the Ruy Lopez opening.

13 Ng5 Rf8
14 Nf3 Re8
Back to the position in the diagram.

15 Ng5 Rf8

16 Nf3 Re8
Back again. Neither side wanted to claim the draw at this point so they played on.

17 Ng5 Rf8
18 Nf3 Na5
19 Bc2 Nc4
20 b3 Nb6
21 Nbd2 Re8
22 dxe5 dxe5
23 Nxe5 Bd6
24 Nef3 Bxe4
25 Nxe4 Nxe4
26 Qd3 f5
27 Be3 Bf8
28 Rad1
And the game now ended in a draw anyway (by mutual agreement; one player offered the draw and the other accepted), even though there are still plenty of pieces on the board. ½ - ½

Fifty-Move Rule

A game is drawn if there are 50 consecutive moves in a game of chess without a pawn move or a capture. Imagine you have a king and a rook and the opponent has just a king. If you don't know the technique to force a checkmate, there is a real possibility that you will end up checking the lone king around the board for a long time without making any progress. After 50 moves (each) the game ends in a draw. The logic of the rule is that if one player can't force checkmate from such an easily winning position in 50 moves, then there is little chance of them ever doing it, so to continue is a waste of time.

Insufficient Material

This can happen at the end of a very tough game between players of a similar standard. If there is no possible way to force a checkmate, then the game is a draw.

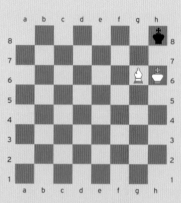

This is a draw, regardless of who is to move. There is no way to force a checkmate even though the black king is in the corner. White needs at least another bishop (on the dark squares) or a knight to help with the checkmate. Even adding a pawn to the h-file won't help White to win.

This is a classic case of insufficient material. Obviously neither side can make any sort of progress here. There are other cases too.

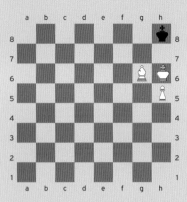

It doesn't matter who is to move here. The game is drawn because White cannot force Black's king out of the corner to enable his pawn to promote. If the white pawn is on any other file, then White will win by promoting his pawn to a queen and then forcing checkmate.

Black to play

This is another draw. White simply cannot protect all of the squares around the black king and check him at the same time. Remarkably, even a position with a king and two knights against a lone king is draw, because the knights are not powerful enough to force the enemy king into a checkmate position. A bishop, knight and king can force checkmate against a lone king, as can two bishops and a king.

The Three Phases of the Game

Once players have mastered the basic moves and worked out how to avoid losing to one of the early checkmates, then their games will gradually become longer and tougher. It cannot be overstated: chess development comes only with a good deal of work, lots of practice and the ability to learn from an abundance of very hard lessons. It is, unfortunately, always necessary to suffer quite a few painful defeats to be able to improve.

The game of chess can be split into three phases:

1) Opening
This is the time to occupy the centre with pawns, develop the minor pieces (knights and bishops), ensure the king is safe (by castling) and then to find the best positions for the queen and rooks.

2) Middlegame
The middlegame is the time when the opposing forces come into contact. Plans are required, rather than simple developing moves, and both players need to be very aware of tactical ideas.

3) Endgame
Not all games reach an endgame. Middlegame attacks will often finish off an opponent. The endgame is characterized by a lack of direct danger to the king. If he can safely enter the battle without fearing checkmate at every turn, then it's safe to assume the endgame has been reached. Endgame strategy mainly revolves around trying to promote a pawn, when the addition of a new queen should prove to be decisive.

To be successful one will need to study each phase of the game carefully.

TACTICAL WEAPONS

Chess players need to develop their own personal stockpile of tactical weapons. The more typical patterns one can remember, the more chance there is of a game ending successfully.

Knowledge of forks, pins, skewers and other devices is essential.

White to play

The Fork

A fork is a move that attacks two or more targets at the same time. Forks can be carried out by any chess piece or pawn.

Here is a basic example of a knight fork.

White's knight seizes the opportunity to fork three pieces with 1 Nxc7+! Black will have to escape from check by moving his king and White can capture the black queen or rook.

Can you see how White can create a fork in each of the following positions?

White to play
Hint: Look for a queen move.

White to play
Hint: Even little pawns can fork big pieces.

The Pin

Pins occur when one piece (or pawn) is under attack but it cannot move (if pinned against the king, because it is illegal to expose the king to check) or it would be bad to move it (if pinned against a piece of higher value).

This is a basic pin.

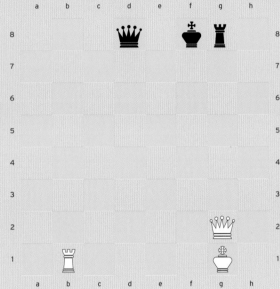

White to play

Black's rook is attacking the queen. The queen cannot move off the g-file because then White's king will be exposed to check. The best White can do is gain the rook for the queen (either now, with 1 Qxg8+ Kxg8, or wait for Black to capture the queen with 1 ...Rxg2+).

Pins can be administered by queens, rooks and bishops. Pins do not always involve the opponent's king and they do not always win material. Sometimes they simply temporarily prevent a piece from moving.

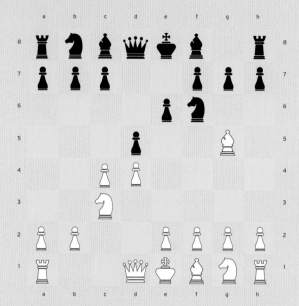

Black to play

In this position, White's bishop is pinning the black knight against the queen. The knight could still move but it is inadvisable because White would then capture the queen. However, the pin is by no means serious. Black can simply play 1 ...Be7, breaking the pin. Now his knight can move if it wants to without any serious consequences. For example, after 2 cxd5 Nxd5, White's bishop can no longer capture the queen and after 3 Bxe7 Black can simply recapture with 3 ...Qxe7 and it's a fair exchange (bishop for bishop).

The Skewer

A skewer is very much like a pin but with the defender's pieces switching roles.

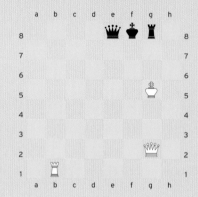

White to play

White's king is in check and it must move off the g-file. Black will then capture the white queen (1 ...Rxg2) and gain a winning advantage.

As with the pin, a skewer doesn't have to include the king.

White to play

Material is equal at the moment but White's queen is under attack and he faces two bad choices. Moving the queen away from the e-file allows 1 ...Rxe1+, winning a whole rook for Black. The best White can do is play 1 Qxe6, when at least he obtains a rook in return for his queen.

Discovered Check

A discovered check happens when one piece moves away and unleashes a check from another piece.

White to play

When White moves the bishop, it will uncover a check on the black king by the rook. Using this discovered check enables him to win the black queen with the move 1 Bd6+. Now imagine if the position featured a black pawn defending the king.

White to play

Without the discovered check, 1 Bd6?? would be met simply by 1 ...Qxd6.

Discovered Attack

Discovered attacks are based on the same idea as discovered checks, only without involving the opponent's king.

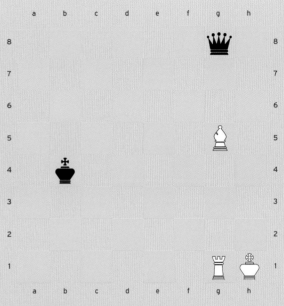

White to play

White has two ways to play a winning discovered attack: 1 Be7+ and 1 Bd2+. Both place the black king in check and both unleash an attack on the black queen by the white rook. White will therefore gain a winning advantage in the game.

Removing the Guard

If one piece is protecting another, it may be possible to chase away or capture the defending piece, leaving the other one exposed to capture.

White to play

White is already winning this position but he can increase his advantage by playing 1 e5. Now the black knight is under attack and if it moves away White can safely capture the bishop. If the bishop moves then White will simply capture the knight instead.

These tactics crop up during all stages of the game and one must remain constantly alert to the possibility of their occurrence. They can be powerful enough to change the whole course of the game, turning a victory into a defeat (or vice versa).

It is essential to become more familiar with the standard chess tactics and their typical patterns. There's certainly no shortage of books full of chess puzzles and it is strongly recommended to work through one or two of them from start to finish.

Here are a few examples for you to test yourself. They are all positions extracted from games played at the **2013 British Chess Championship**. The solutions are given at the back of the book.

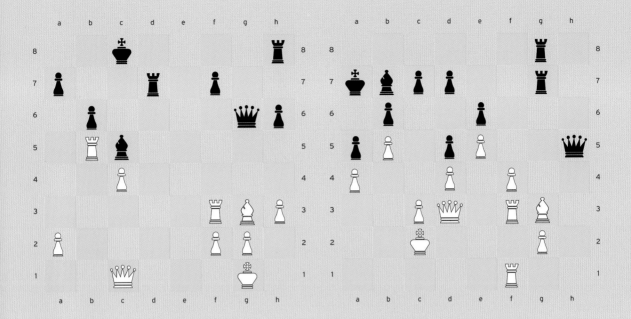

Gawain Jones vs. John Reid
White to play

Alan Brusey vs. Charles Storey
Black to play

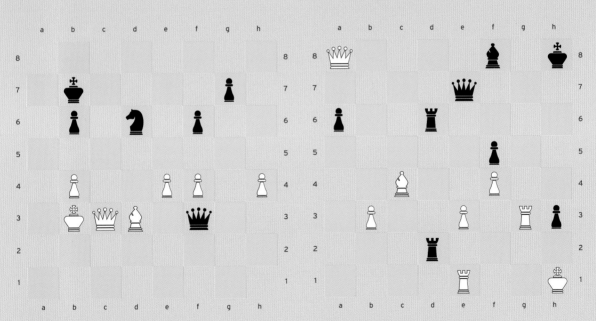

Mark Hebden vs. Colin Purdon
White to play

David Howell vs. Jack Rudd
White to play

Richard Bates vs. Sarah Hegarty
White to play

Peter Mercs vs. Thomas Thorpe
White to play

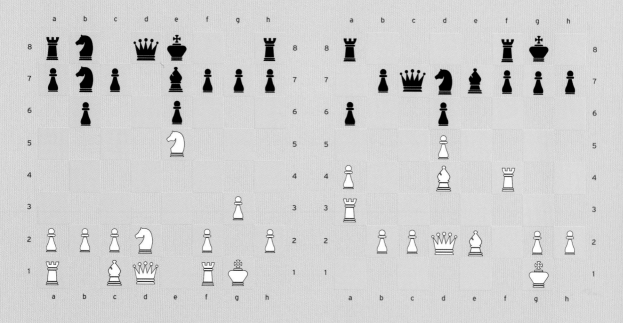

Ameet Ghasi vs. Gyula Meszaros
White to play

Gawain Jones vs. Donald Mason
White to play

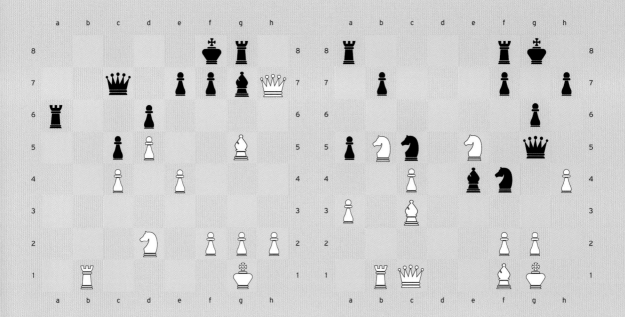

Gawain Jones vs. Terry Chapman
White to play

Dominic Mackle vs. Gawain Jones
Black to play

Sarah Hegarty vs. Liam Varnam
White to play

Alexander Longson vs. Richard Palliser
Black to play

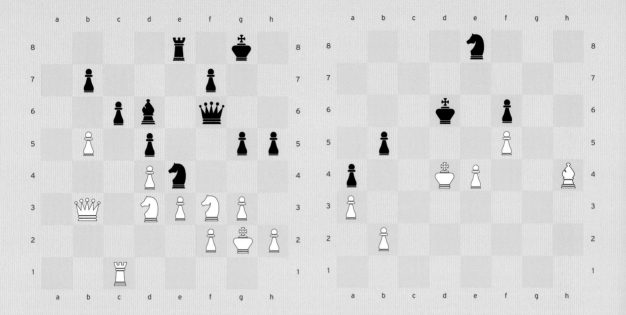

Daniel Fernandez vs. Peter Wells
Black to play

David Eggleston vs. Sarah Hegarty
White to play

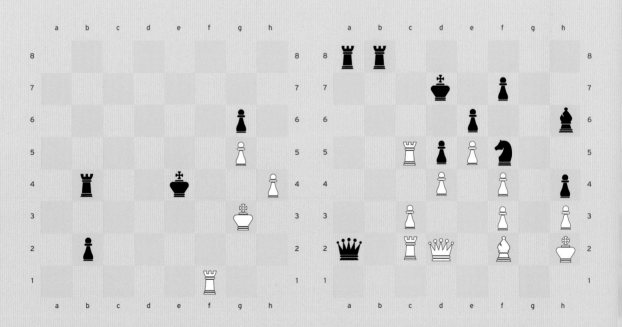

Charles Storey vs. Colin Purdon
White to play

Jasper Tambini vs. Neil Carr
Black to play

Tactical Weapons in Detail

As the game of chess always starts with the same pieces and the same rules, one could be forgiven for thinking that there is little scope for individual flair. Yet quite the opposite is true! It is remarkable how chess players are able to impose their personalities and preferences on the board.

Some players have a liking for quiet, positional play. They prefer to keep control over what is happening on the board and seek to win by patiently accumulating small advantages. Others prefer to engage directly with the opponent and like to create tactical situations as soon as possible, confident that their knowledge of tactical weapons and powers of calculation will serve them well. They are quite prepared to take risks, often sacrificing material in their quest to win quickly.

Of course, each game of chess can only be won once. Tournaments don't award extra points for quick, tactical victories any more than they do for lengthy positional battles. It is purely a matter of taste.

Chess players will develop their own style as their experience grows. It is useful to study the games of great players to assist such development.

We present some samples from the heroes. Please look carefully at the examples from their games to compare their respective styles. Whose style of play best matches your own?

Of all the World Champions, Mikhail Tal, 'Misha' to one and all, was the most liked, admired and, yes, loved by colleagues and chess fans the world over.

YASSER SEIRAWAN, IN CHESS DUELS.

Hero of Tactical Play – Mikhail Tal

Our hero for tactical play is Mikhail Tal. His extraordinary tactical ability allowed him to sweep aside the best players in the world on his way to becoming World Champion at the first attempt. When he defeated Mikhail Botvinnik to take the title in 1960, Tal became the youngest world champion in history at the age of 23 (a record broken 25 years later by Garry Kasparov).

Tal specialized in sacrificing pawns and pieces to create enormous complications on the board. He remained true to his style regardless of the strength of the opposition and was universally admired by chess fans across the world.

To be able to demolish less experienced opponents with a cascade of sacrifices is one thing, but to do it on a regular basis against the world's elite was a phenomenal achievement.

R.TEŠNERS M.TĀLS
VFR   PSRS

He was a man in whose presence others sensed their mediocrity.

GARRY KASPAROV, RADIO INTERVIEW.

Here are some stunning examples of Tal in action.

Mikhail Tal vs. Georgi Tringov
Interzonal tournament, Amsterdam, 1964

Tal's explosive style produced numerous quick wins, including this one.

1 e4 g6
2 d4 Bg7
3 Nc3 d6
4 Nf3 c6
5 Bg5 Qb6

This looks like a bad choice of opening against Tal. Once he had an advantage in development he would automatically look for ways to complicate the position. With his next move he offers the first sacrifice of the game.

6 Qd2 Qxb2

Black is a pawn up but White has lots of pieces in action and can gain time for more development by attacking the foolhardy queen.

7 Rb1 Qa3
8 Bc4 Qa5
9 0-0 e6
10 Rfe1

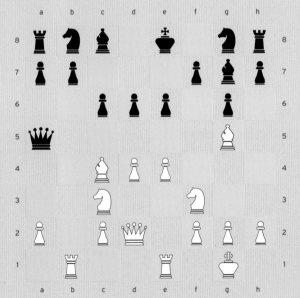

All of White's pieces are in play and his king is very safe. Black has wasted time moving little else apart from his queen and pawns. It is no wonder that Tal made short work of this game.

10 ...a6
11 Bf4 e5

Black's best move was probably 11 ...Qc7, to defend the d6-pawn. Opening the centre is a fatal mistake.

12 dxe5 dxe5

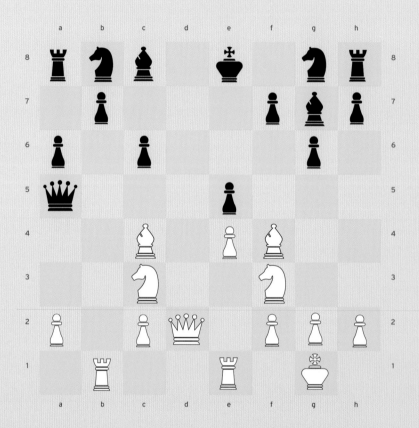

Where will Tal move his bishop? Nowhere! Instead, he offers Black a choice of pieces to capture.

13 Qd6! Qxc3

13 ...exf4 14 Nd5! (threatening 15 Nc7+, when Black would have to give up his queen) exd5 15 exd5+ shows the problems facing Black. His king cannot escape from the centre and Tal's pieces are swarming around like angry bees.

14 Red1 Nd7

Black had to defend against the threat of 15 Qd8 checkmate. Tal has another sacrifice up his sleeve...

15 Bxf7+!

15 ...Kxf7

Declining the sacrifice with 15 ...Kd8 runs into a forced checkmate, starting with 16 Ng5.

16 Ng5+ Ke8

17 Qe6+

Checkmate cannot be prevented. 17 ...Kd8 18 Nf7+ Kc7 19 Qd6 mate would have been a particularly pretty finish.

Black resigned instead.

1-0

Mikhail Tal vs. Eduard Meduna
Germany, 1989

1 e4 c6

The solid Caro-Kann Defence is normally a good opening to play against attacking players, but it fails to keep Tal quiet in this game.

2 d4 d5
3 Nd2 dxe4
4 Nxe4 Nd7
5 Ng5
5 ...Ngf6

Attempting to chase away the knight with 5 ...h6 can lead to very early complications after 6 Ne6! The point is that 6 ...fxe6 fails to 7 Qh5+ g6 8 Qxg6 checkmate and if he avoids that trap then he has to decide where to move his queen. Nobody would want to have to solve such early problems against Tal.

6 Bd3 c5
7 N1f3 cxd4

Most players would be tempted to simply recapture the pawn here with 8 Nxd4 but Tal – as usual – prefers rapid development to material considerations.

8 0-0 Qb6

Black hopes to exploit Tal's idea by holding on to the pawn for as long as possible. 8 ...e5 looks natural, protecting the pawn and establishing a pawn centre, but it fails to 9 Bc4! and the f7 square will collapse, taking Black's game with it.

9 Bc4 e6
10 Re1 Be7

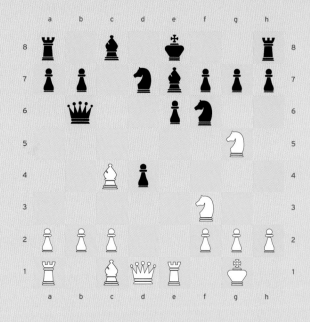

An obvious developing move, but it's a bad one as it allows one of Tal's trademark sacrifices. 10... Nc5 was a better move – unblocking the queen's bishop and allowing it defend the e-pawn – but White would still have the advantage.

11 Nxf7!

Just the sort of position one *wouldn't* want to have against Tal. 11 ...Kxf7 12 Rxe6 is too horrible to contemplate but Black is struggling whatever he decides to play.

11 ...Qc7
12 Bxe6 Nc5

Sensibly trying to relieve some of the pressure through exchanges, but Tal keeps the pieces on.

13 Bc4 b5

An attempt to deflect the bishop from its defence of the knight (14 Bxb5+? Kxf7 gives Black a little bit of hope).

14 Qxd4! bxc4
15 Bf4

It is instructive to see how Tal invariably finds ways to bring even more pressure to bear on an opponent's position.

15 ...Qb6
16 Nxh8 Be6
17 Ng5 Rd8

18 Qe3, 18 Qc3 and 18 Qe5 are all very sensible ways to keep the queen safe and preserve a huge advantage, but Tal just keeps the sacrifices going.

18 Qxc5!

A queen sacrifice! Tal has worked out that the threats from his remaining pieces are simply too strong for Black to cope with. If now 18... Bxc5 19 Rxe6+ wins back the queen with a big material advantage.

18 ...Qxc5
19 Nxe6 Qb6
20 Bc7

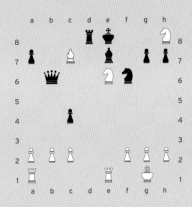

Black to play

Black needs to move his queen and 20 ...Qxb2 is the best try. That would lead to the following variation: 20 ...Qxb2 21 Bxd8 Bxd8 22 Rad1 Be7 23 Nc7+ Kf8 24 Rb1.

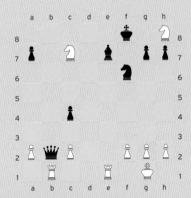

Analysis diagram

If Black wants to keep his queen it will have to move off the b-file, but then White will force a checkmate with 25 Rb8+ Bd8 26 Rxd8+ Ne8 27 R(any)xe8 checkmate. Black resigned instead.
1-0

Each of the following positions provides a further demonstration of Tal's attacking flair.

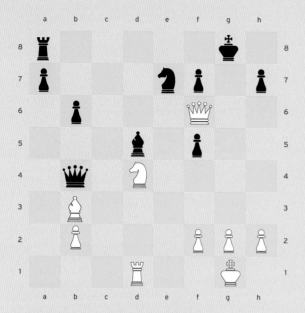

Mikhail Tal vs. Alexander Tolush
USSR Championship, Riga, 1958
White to play

Tal is a pawn down, but that's not an important factor. Black's king is in a weak position (compare the wall of pawns in front of White's king, keeping it safe, with the shattered structure in front of the black king). Tal has four active pieces; Tolush's rook is sitting in the corner and cannot influence matters in the centre of the board. Tal's next move must have come as a total surprise.

25 Nc6!

At first glance this looks like a ridiculous move, offering Black a choice of taking either the knight or the bishop. However, in reality, Black's choices are all bad and his position is lost.

His options are:
25 ...Bxb3 which just loses the queen after 26 Nxb4.
25 ...Nxc6 which allows 26 Bxd5, pinning the knight against the rook, at the same time as *forking* the knight and the f7-pawn. Black will lose

at least the knight.
25 ...Bxc6 which is even worse. White would simply play 26 Qxf7+ Kh8 27 Qf6 checkmate. In the game, Tolush finds another way to capture a piece, but he doesn't last much longer.

25 ...Qxb3
26 Nxe7+ Kf8
27 Re1

Defending the knight and threatening 28 Qh8 checkmate.

27 ...Be6

Now 28 Qh8+ would win the exchange after 28 ...Kxe7 29 Qxa8 but Tal sees a way to force checkmate instead.

28 Nxf5

If 28 ...Bxf5, then 29 Qh8 is checkmate. Any normal-looking move (for example, 28 ...Rc8) allows the same checkmate (29 Qh8). So Black resigned.
1-0

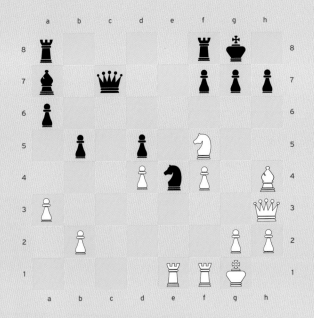

Mikhail Tal vs. Miguel Najdorf
Chess Olympiad, Leipzig, 1960
White to play

It is easy to see that Tal is limbering up for an attack on the black king. He has a queen, two rooks, a bishop and a knight all pointing in that direction. Najdorf has a passive rook in the corner (just as Tolush did in the previous game) and a bishop that is currently shut out of the action. Black's knight is in a very good position but it doesn't stay there for very long.

21 Rxe4! dxe4
Tal has *sacrificed the exchange* to remove Black's best placed piece and to weaken the defence of the king.

22 Bf6!
Exploiting the fact that the knight is no longer defending the f6 square. If Black accepts the bishop sacrifice with 22 ...gxf6 he loses quickly to 23 Qg4+ (or 23 Qg3+) Kh8 24 Qg7 checkmate.

22 ...Qb6
Black's best reply, threatening to capture the bishop with the queen in order to keep the pawn wall intact. If White has to meekly retreat the bishop then Black will gain the advantage, as he will be the exchange ahead and will have repulsed the attack.

23 Bxg7!
Shattering the defensive wall in front of Black's king.

23 ...Rfe8
24 Be5 Qg6
Black is trying to plug the gaps in his defence but Tal very rarely failed to land a blow against a weakened king.

25 Nh6+ Kf8

26 f5
The finishing touch. Black's defence now collapses under the pressure. If he tries to keep the queen active by 26 ...Qg5, White will sacrifice again with 27 Nxf7! Kxf7 28 Qxh7+ Kf8 29 Bd6+ Re7 30 f6 with an easy win. So Najdorf decided to resign.
1-0

**Mikhail Tal vs.
John van der Wiel**
*Interzonal tournament,
Moscow, 1982
White to play*

Black hasn't castled - a risky policy against Tal. 19 Nf6+ is tempting, but Black's king is relatively safe after 19 ...Kd8. Tal found a typical sacrifice...

19 Rxf7!
Tearing away a key defensive pawn, but it costs a rook! If White's attack fails then Black will win easily.

19 ...Kxf7
20 Qf6+ Kg8
20 ...Ke8? allows 21 Qxh8+ with an easy win for White.

21 Qxe7 Rf8

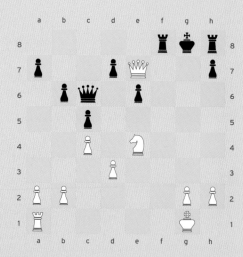

22 Rf1!
A brilliant and unexpected finishing touch. If 22 ...Rxf1+ 23 Kxf1 there is no sensible defence to 24 Nf6+ checkmate. 22 ...Rf5 is the best try but Tal would still force checkmate after 23 Nf6+! Rxf6 24 Rxf6 with checkmate by either 25 Qf7 or 25 Rf8 to follow. Black resigned. **1-0**

Play Like Tal!

Now you are familiar with Tal's sacrificial style, perhaps you can finish off some of his games for him? Try to find the winning moves in the following positions. You will find the solutions at the back of the book.

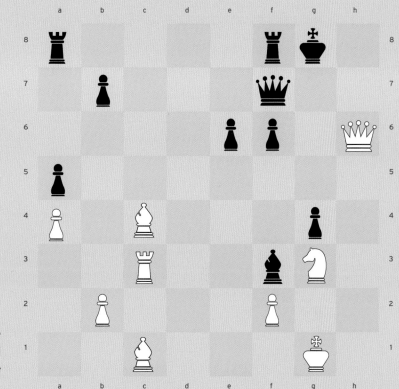

Mikhail Tal vs. Bob Wade
Tallinn, 1971
White to play

Mikhail Tal vs. Peter Kiriakov
Latvian Championship, 1965
White to play

Mikhail Tal vs. Jan Timman
Chess Olympiad, Skopje, 1972
White to play

POSITIONAL PLAY

Positional play is harder to categorize than tactical play but there are some basic ideas one should always keep in mind.

1) Improve the position of your pieces. If your position has a badly placed piece then you will need to look for ways to improve it.

2) Place your rooks on open (or half-open) files. By doing this your rooks will enjoy more scope and may be able to invade the enemy position.

3) Pay particular attention to pawn structures. Keep your own structure healthy and try to inflict damage on that of your opponent.

Black to play

Positional Play in Detail

A large amount of good positional play revolves around improving the positions of the pieces. One badly placed piece can result in the whole position suffering for a long period of time. A bad piece is one lacking in scope and immediate prospects.

Improving the Bishops

Bishops are long range pieces. They don't like cramped positions or being obstructed by pawns.

In this position, Black's queen's bishop (on c8) is in danger of becoming a bad piece. It will have problems coming out to the good squares f5 and g4, because its development is hindered by the pawn on e6. Black cannot rely on White relieving the situation with cxd5 exd5, when the bishop can easily be developed, so Black needs an alternative plan. Playing

7 ...Bd7 is not so good, as the bishop won't have any useful moves after that, and furthermore the queen's knight might like to use the d7 square. The simplest way to solve the problem is to play 7 ...b6, followed by 8...Bb7 and 9 ...dxc4. The specific moves could be:

7 ...b6
8 Bd3 Bb7
9 0-0 dxc4
10 Bxc4

Black to play

This is a standard position from an opening called the Grunfeld Defence (reached after 1 d4 Nf6 2 c4 g6 3 Nc3 d5 4 cxd5 Nxd5 5 e4 Nxc3 6 bxc3 Bg7 7 Bc4). The black king's bishop would like to have more scope but it is currently impeded by White's strong pawn centre. The d4-pawn is well protected and will not move voluntarily. Black's plan must be to try to break down the pawns on d4 and c3 and thereby unleash his bishop. Typical moves from this position are:

Black to play

On comparing the two diagrams, it should be easy to see that Black has greatly improved the position and prospects of his queen's bishop.

If bishops are blocked by strong pawns belonging to the opponent then a plan must be found to undermine them.

7 ...c5
Tempting White to capture a pawn, but the consequences would be terrible: 8 dxc5?? Bxc3+ and Black's bishop has achieved its objective. It is forking the white king and rook and 9 ...Bxa1 cannot be prevented.

8 Ne2
Just as Black's plan is based on unleashing his potentially powerful bishop, so White's plan is to keep it blocked in, so he rushes to strengthen the d-pawn. 8 Nf3 looks natural and seems to be a

better square for the knight, but then Black could play 8 ...Bg4, pinning the knight and thus greatly increasing the pressure on the d4 square.

8 ...Nc6

Another good developing move, once again applying pressure to White's d-pawn.

9 Be3

Developing the bishop and yet again protecting d4.

9 ...0-0

Safeguarding the king before further action is undertaken.

9 0-0

Both players have produced moves consistent with their positional plans. The struggle will continue along the same lines, with Black exerting more pressure on the white centre and White trying hard to keep control. Two good options for Black are 9 ...Qc7 (to play 10 ...Rd8, with even more pressure on the d-pawn) and 9 ...Bg4 (pinning the white knight to reduce its influence on the centre and tempting White to chase away the bishop with 10 f3, which leaves potential weaknesses on the black squares).

Improving the Rooks

Where do rooks belong? On open files!

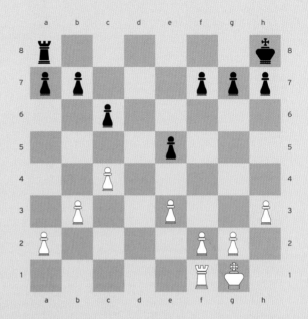

White to play

Any experienced player would immediately play 1 Rd1 here, without thinking about any other moves. Taking total control of the only open file gives White a large advantage, probably enough eventually to win the game. Black's problems become more apparent after just a couple of moves.

1 Rd1 Kg8
2 Rd7

Establishing a rook on the seventh rank is an excellent achievement and usually a sign of a great advantage. Black now has to solve major problems. How is he going to keep all of his pawns safe and how can he possibly force the white rooks out of his position? He can wait passively and play **2 ...Rb8** to defend his pawn, but he will just have to sit and watch as White gradually increases his advantage by bringing his king into the game.

One rook on the seventh rank is very strong; two rooks on the seventh rank often win very quickly, as in the following game.

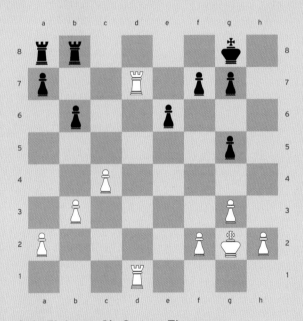

Salo Flohr vs. Sir George Thomas
Hastings, 1937
White to play

Salo Flohr was a great positional player. Here, material is currently equal but Flohr doesn't miss the chance to gain a big advantage by placing both of his rooks on the seventh rank.

25 Re7
Making way for the other rook to occupy d7.

25 ...a5
Black would like to oppose the rook and challenge for control of the open file with 25 ...Rd8, but he would lose a pawn after 26 Rxd8+ Rxd8 27 Rxa7 (or even 26 Rxa7 first) and White's rook would still dominate the position. Thomas tries to safeguard his pawns before attempting to deal with the invading rooks.

26 Rdd7

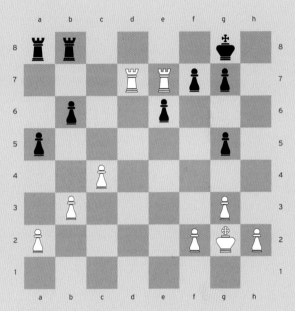

White is threatening to sweep across the seventh rank and wipe out all of Black's kingside pawns, one after the other.

26 ...Rf8
Protecting the f-pawn.

27 Rb7 Ra6
A clumsy way of using the rook to defend the b-pawn, but the alternative 27 ...Rab8 allows White to win more material with the clever 28 Rxf7!

Analysis diagram

28 a4

A good move to emphasize White's dominance. Black may have been planning to play 28 ...a4, with the hope of improving the position of his queen's rook, but now he can't move the pawn at all. Unable to find a single good move, Thomas resigned this position.

1-0

Improving the Knight

Unlike bishops, the short-range knights enjoy closed positions. They can jump over pieces and pawns and it is not easy to keep them out of the action for long. They have more power the closer they are to the centre of the board.

If a knight is poorly placed it is definitely worth taking the time needed to improve its position. This is a classic example.

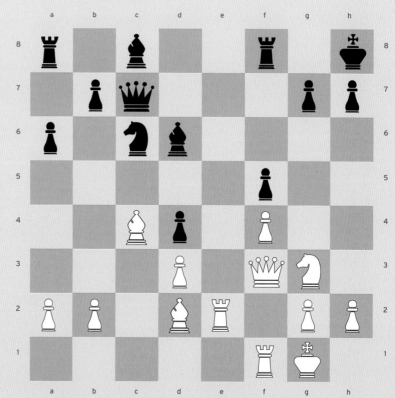

Aaron Nimzowitsch vs. Akiva Rubinstein
Dresden, 1926
White to play

White's knight is in a bad position and it lacks prospects. Nimzowitsch, one of the greatest original thinkers in the history of chess, came up with a very instructive plan to bring the knight back into the game.

18 Nh1!!

Knights are usually at their worst when forced into corners but Nimzowitsch has found a safe path for its speedy return to action. The knight hopes to travel to g5 via f2 and h3.

18 ...Bd7
19 Nf2 Rae8
20 Rfe1 Rxe2
21 Rxe2 Nd8
22 Nh3

Not much has happened since the previous diagram although clearly the knight is slowly but surely heading for a better place.

22 ...Bc6

If Black played to exchange the rooks with 22 ... Re8 then the first idea behind White's planned knight tour would have been revealed in style, i.e. 23 Qh5 Rxe2 24 Ng5!! h6 (to stop 25 Qxh7 checkmate) 25 Qg6! (renewing the threat of checkmate on h7) 25 ...hxg5 26 Qh5 checkmate.

Analysis diagram

23 Qh5 g6
24 Qh4 Kg7
25 Qf2 Bc5
26 b4 Bb6
27 Qh4 Re8
28 Re5 Nf7
29 Bxf7 Qxf7
30 Ng5

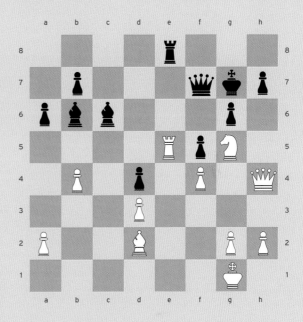

It took some time for the knight to get g5 but it was worth it. Black's defence is creaking under the strain; he has serious concerns about the attacks on e8, f7 and h7.

30 ...Qg8
31 Rxe8 Bxe8
32 Qe1 Bc6
33 Qe7+ Kh8

Nimzowitsch's knight is now a very powerful piece. Rubinstein needs to keep a very careful eye on the h7 and f7 points, so his queen is tied down for the duration. But how is White going to introduce more energy into the attack?

34 b5!!

Nimzowitsch follows up his exemplary lesson in how to improve the position of a knight with an equally instructive example of how to activate a sleeping bishop.

34 ...Qg7

Rubinstein offers an exchange of queens in a bid to escape from the mating attack. It does cost him a bishop, so the end is merely delayed. He was short of serious alternatives. 34 ...Bxb5 loses a bishop to 35 Qf6+ and 36 Qxb6. 34 ...axb5 fails to the main idea, which comes after 35 Ne6 (threatening 36 Qf6+ Qg7 37 Qxg7 checkmate) 35 ...h5 (to give the king a flight square) 36 Qf6+ Kh7 37 Ng5+ Kh6 38 Bb4! with the winning intention of 39 Bf8+. 35 ...h6, to keep the white knight out of g5, also loses quickly: 36 Qf6+ Kh7 37 Nf8+ and the only way for Black to get out of check is to give up his queen with 37 ...Qxf8.

35 Qxg7+ Kxg7
36 bxc6 bxc6

White to play

Rubinstein has only one pawn in return for the extra white knight. The rest is very easy for Nimzowitsch.

37 Nf3

Not that it matters much at this stage, but the best move here was 37 Bb4, preventing Black from connecting his pawns with 37 ...c5. The point is that 37 Bb4 c5?? loses more material to 38 Bxc5! Bxc5 39 Ne6+ with a knight fork, followed by 40 Nxc5 once Black escapes from check.

37 ...c5
38 Ne5 Bc7
39 Nc4 Kf7
40 g3 Bd8
41 Ba5 Be7
42 Bc7 Ke6
43 Nb6 h6
44 h4 g5
45 h5 g4
46 Be5
1-0

Improving the King

The position of the king is of paramount importance during every phase of the game. In the opening there is a very easy way to improve your position – by castling, which every player should aim to carry out as soon as possible. If the king is left insufficiently defended early on in the game, then the chances are he will not survive for very long. In the middlegame, the king must be kept safe from the opponent's tactical ideas.

Garry Kasparov had a habit of taking a move to improve the position of his king just before launching a big attack. The idea is to ensure his king isn't hit by a stray check at an inconvenient moment. This is well worth remembering.

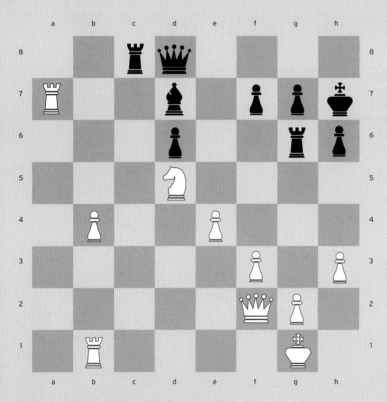

Garry Kasparov vs. Anatoly Karpov
Game 18, World Championship Match, 1990
White to play

Kasparov's excellent, centralized knight and extra pawn give him a clear advantage. Karpov may have some counter chances due to his rook pinning the g2-pawn against Kasparov's king, and ...Bxh3 may be on the cards at some point. Kasparov's next move eliminates a considerable amount of the danger.

38 Kh2!
Calmly unpinning the g2-pawn and remaining on a black square to avoid any future checks by Karpov's bishop. White's king suddenly looks much safer and he can proceed with his winning plan of utilizing his extra space and material.

38 ...Rb8
39 f4 Re6
40 Qd4 Qe8
41 Re1 Bc6
42 Qd3!

Black is forced to think carefully about defence. Kasparov's last move aimed to meet 42 ...Bxd5?? with 43 exd5+, attacking the rook on e6. The rook could block the check and save itself at the same time with 43 ...Rg6 but then 44 Rxe8 gives White an easy win.

42 ...Qf8
43 Rc1 Bxd5
44 exd5+ Rg6
45 Qf5 Kg8
46 Rac7 Rf6
47 Qd7 Rd8

Karpov is defending very stubbornly but Kasparov finds an effective simplification.

48 Qxd8!
A very temporary sacrifice. Kasparov will quickly win back the queen with a pin.

48 ...Qxd8
49 Rc8 Qf8
50 R1c4 Rf5
51 Rxf8+ Kxf8
52 Rd4 h5
53 b5 Ke7
54 b6 Kd7
55 g4 hxg4
56 hxg4 Rf6
57 Rc4

Kasparov's passed b-pawn will decide the game. The best try for Karpov would be 57 ...Rh6+ 58 Kg2 Rh8 but then 59 Rc7+! Kd8 60 Ra7! followed by a skewer (61 Ra8+ winning the black rook) or pawn promotion (60 ...Rh4 61 Ra8+ Kd7 62 b7, with b8=Q to follow). Karpov resigned.
1-0

Two games later, in the same match, Kasparov used the same idea again.

Garry Kasparov vs. Anatoly Karpov
Game 20, World Championship Match, 1990
White to play

The position is terribly complicated and both kings could be in serious trouble. Kasparov would like to move his knight but doesn't want to allow ...Qxe1+. If the capture was not being made with check, there wouldn't be such a problem, so he safely tucks away his king.

31 Kh2! Qe5
32 Ng5!

Black to play

This is the big idea. The knight joins the attack in decisive fashion and 32 ...Qxe1 isn't a problem as it does not check the white king. Kasparov would simply play 33 Nf7 checkmate. At the same time, Black's queen is under attack and she must protect the f7 square.

32 ...Qf6
33 ...Qg7 allows 34 Qxh6+!! intending 34 ...Qxh6 35 Nf7 checkmate.

33 Re8 Bf5
Karpov's position now suffers the full force of a tactical whirlwind.

34 Qxh6+ Qxh6
35 Nf7+ Kh7
36 Bxf5+ Qg6
37 Bxg6+ Kg7
38 Rxa8 Be7
39 Rb8 a5
40 Be4+ Kxf7
41 Bxd5+

Kasparov's material advantage is massive and Karpov resigned at this point.
1-0

Nudging the king into safety just before the final phase of the game became a Kasparov speciality. Here's another example, against the man who would eventually replace him as World Champion.

Garry Kasparov vs. Vladimir Kramnik
Linares, 1997
White to play

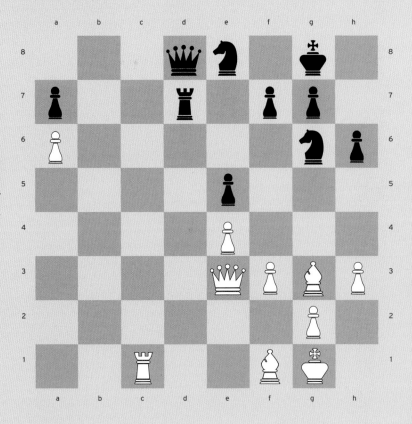

40 Kh2!
With his king tucked away safely from any trouble, Kasparov can use his bishop pair and more active pieces to improve his position. He will then exploit his extra space to apply more pressure on Kramnik's position, with a view to winning material. The target is the a7-pawn.

	40 ...Re7
41 Rc6	Kh7
42 Qc1	Nc7
43 Qc3	Qd7
44 Rc5	Qd6
45 Bf2	Ne6
46 Rd5	Qb8
47 Rb5	Qd6
48 Rb7	Nd4
49 Qb4	Qf6
50 Qc5	Nc6
51 Be3	Re6
52 Bc4	Re7
53 Bd5	Nd4

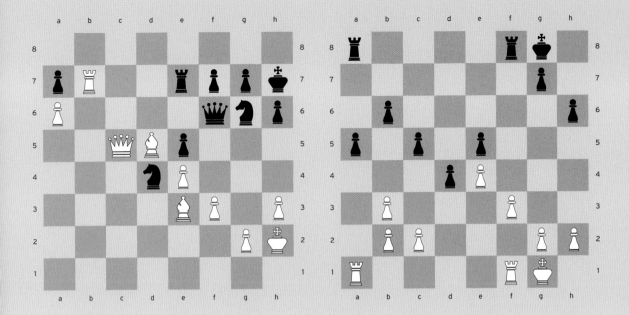

Kasparov now picks up the pawn and the game heads for a rapid conclusion

54 Rxa7 Rxa7
55 Qxa7 Ne7
56 Bc4 h5
57 Qc5

Black's position is hopeless. Kramnik resigned.
1-0

In each of the examples it is very noticeable how safe Kasparov's king was after Kh2.

Kings generally enjoy the endgame much more than other phases of the game. The danger of checkmate diminishes when most of the pieces have been exchanged and the king can have a decisive influence on the outcome of a game.

The brilliant José Raul Capablanca (World Champion, 1921-27) excelled at the endgame and there are numerous examples of his exemplary technique. In the following example his king heads towards the centre of the board, from where it conducts the final phase of the battle with great aplomb.

Lis Molina Carranza vs. José Raul Capablanca
Exhibition Game, Buenos Aires, 1911
Black to play

23 ...Kf7
24 Kf2 Ke6
25 Ke2 b5
26 Kd2 g5
27 h3 h5
28 g4 h4

Capablanca's king is well placed and he is gradually seizing more space. A quick comparison between the previous diagram and the next one should be enough to see how Black's position has improved.

29 Ke2 Rf7
30 Rf2 Rfa7

Preparing a timely break on the queenside.

31 Kd3 a4
32 bxa4 c4+!

Nudging the White king away from the action. Capablanca rarely missed a chance to improve his position.

33 Kd2 Rxa4
34 Rb1 Ra1
35 Rff1 Rxb1
36 Rxb1 Ra2
37 Kd1 b4
38 Kd2

White is hanging on by his fingertips. The black king now steps in to apply even more pressure. It is important to understand how safe the king is in such an endgame. Marching him across the board involves no risk whatsoever.

38 ...Kd6!
39 Kd1 Kc5
40 b3 c3
41 Rc1

If White can play 42 Ke2 then his position will be very difficult to crack, but Capablanca now makes use of a standard sacrifice.

41 ...d3!

Capablanca's rook will now be activated along the seventh rank.

42 cxd3 Rh2
43 Rc2 Rh1+
44 Ke2 Kd4

White has been tied up in knots. It is indicative of the seriousness of his problems when one considers that 45 f4 is his best move (45 Kf2, for example, loses the rook after 45 ...Rh2+ and 46 ...Rxc2). After 45 f4 Rh2+ 46 Kd1 Rxc2 47 Kxc2 exf4 Black will quickly promote a pawn with an easily winning position. White chose to resign at this point.

0-1

The next example shows a truly remarkable king march.

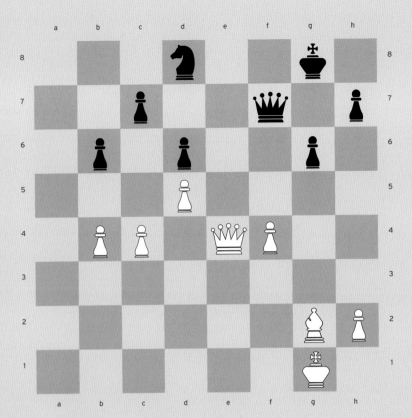

Paul Keres vs. Erich Eliskases
Prague, 1937
White to play

Paul Keres is one of the strongest players who never won the title of World Champion. He was certainly strong enough to do so but suffered various misfortunes at key moments in chess history. In this game, the position is balanced. White's bishop is stronger than the knight (it is more active) but he has a potentially weak pawn on f4 (it cannot be protected by another pawn). It's not so easy to come up with any sort of winning plan. Keres shows his class with an extraordinary raid on Black's queenside.

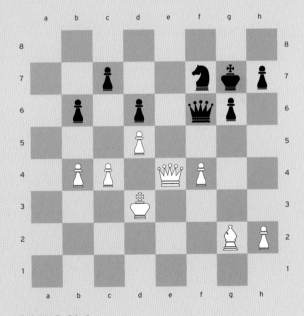

31 Kf2
The start of a long journey.

31 ...Kg7
32 Ke3 Qf6
33 Kd3 Nf7
Keres has centralized his king, in the style of Capablanca, but what is his plan?

34 Kc2 Qh4
35 Kb3 Qxh2
36 Ka4 Qh4
37 Kb5

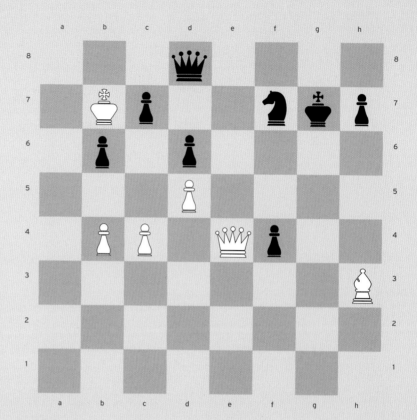

Amazingly, Keres is sending his king to attack Black's queenside pawns and is even prepared to sacrifice a kingside pawn to achieve his objective. Eliskases now brings his queen back home to protect his pawns against the marauding king.

37 ...Qd8
38 Bh3 g5
39 Kc6 gxf4
40 Kb7

40 ...Ne5?!

Eliskases misses his chance. 40 ...Ng5! would have put White to the test, as 41 Qd4+ Qf6 42 Qg1 (pinning the knight) leaves Black with the advantage, although he still has to be very careful about losing his queenside pawns to White's king. After 40 ...Ne5?! Keres is able to continue his queenside play.

41 c5 bxc5

41 ...dxc5?? would lose the knight to 42 Qxe5+.

42 bxc5 Nd7

Bringing the knight back to defend and also threatening a terrible fork with 43 ...Nxc5+!

43 Qd4+

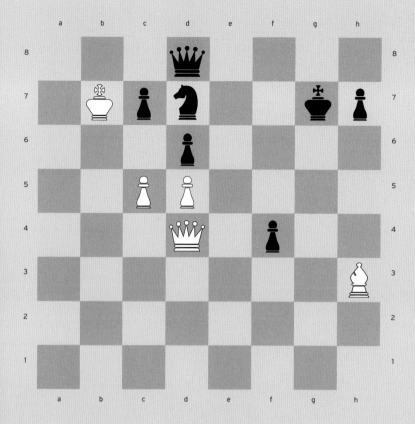

Faced with a wide choice of moves to get out of check, Eliskases picks the worst of all.

43 ...Qf6??
He should have covered with his knight on either f6 or e5. Moving the king – to g6, for example – was also much better than interposing with the queen. Eliskases will now lose his knight!

44 Qg1+! Kf8
45 Bxd7
Keres now has a winning position. A player of his calibre is unlikely to let victory slip when he is a piece up.

45 ...dxc5
46 Qxc5+ Qd6
47 Qxd6+ cxd6
48 Kc7 Ke7
49 Bg4 h6
50 Bf3

Eliskases resigned here. The white bishop is perfectly placed to capture the pawns if they advance (50 ...h5 51 Bxh5 f3 52 Bxf3) and a king move will lose the d-pawn (50 ...Kf6 51 Kxd6 and White's d-pawn will soon be promoted to a queen). The king march ensured the monarch would be in just the right place at the right time.
1-0

Pawn Play

Before the 1700s, pawns were not considered to be important. They were more often than not seen as fodder to be sacrificed at the earliest opportunity to enable the pieces to be developed as quickly as possible. Attack was the order of the day and it was common for both kings to be left hopelessly exposed as the two opponents desperately vied with each other to be the first to deliver a checkmate.

Some of the earliest recorded games of chess feature the Italian, Gioachino Greco, a player noted for his attacking skill.

Gioacchino Greco vs. Anonymous
Europe, 1620

1 e4

Although some early games do commence with 1 d4, the big favourite of the time was definitely 1 e4. Queens came out quickly in those days and the art of positional chess was totally undeveloped.

1 ...e5
2 Bc4 Bc5
3 Qe2 Qe7

Some of the moves seem distinctly odd to the modern eye.

4 f4

This makes it a sort of King's Gambit. The opening is normally reached by 1 e4 e5 2 f4 but even in that form it is rarely played by modern Grandmasters. White's idea is to sacrifice a pawn to tempt the opponent to leave the centre.

4 ...exf4

Another feature of games from this era is a marked reluctance to decline any sort of sacrifice. It was probably regarded as cowardly for a player to avoid the sharpest lines of play.

5 Nf3 g5
6 h4 f6

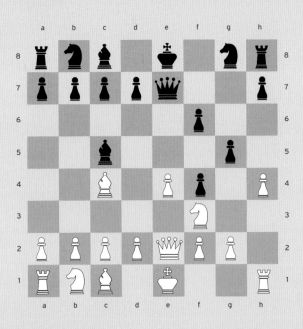

Neither king will be safe on the kingside.
7 hxg5 fxg5
8 Nc3 c6
9 d4 g4

Defensive play is not on the agenda. Black meets fire with fire.

10 Nh4 Bxd4
11 Nf5 Bxc3+
12 bxc3 Qf6
13 Bxf4 Qxc3+
14 Kf2 b5
15 Bb3 a5
16 Nd6+ Kd8
17 Qxg4 Ne7

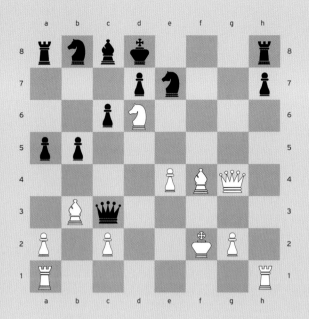

Both kings are in trouble but Greco's is the safer of the two because Black is only attacking with one piece and White is attacking with several.

18 Nf7+ Ke8
19 Qh5 Qd4+
20 Kf3 Qc3+
21 Ke2 Rf8
22 Nd6+ Kd8

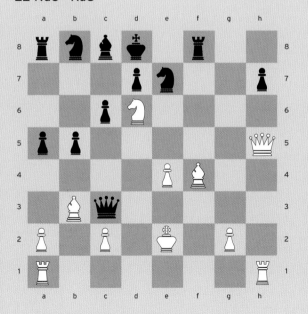

23 Qe8+! Rxe8

23 ...Kc7 is better but 24 Qxf8 would leave Greco with an enormous material advantage. As played, we see a pretty finish.

24 Nf7 checkmate

Checkmate!
Greco's games always provide entertainment and often display instructive checkmate patterns. Yet from a positional point of view it is clear that many improvements can be made. Over 100 years after the Greco game, the great French player, François André Danican Philidor, revolutionized chess thinking and brought attention to the importance of pawns. He called them "the soul of chess" and through his games he showed that they are much too important to fritter away and that a good pawn structure has a very important bearing on the entire game.

Philidor used his pawns to cramp his opponents' positions and demonstrated how the pieces could act very harmoniously in conjunction with a strong pawn structure. His association with pawn structures led to the opening moves 1 e4 e5 2 Nf3 d6 being named Philidor's Defence.

**George Atwood vs.
François André Danican Philidor**

London, 1794

1 e4

Philidor was so much better than his contemporaries that he usually had to offer opponents some compensatory advantage at the start of a game. He frequently played at 'odds of pawn and move', giving his opponents the white pieces, an extra move and an extra pawn too (he removed his f-pawn before the game began). In this game he played 'blindfold', which means Atwood played with the pieces in front of him, as normal, but Philidor had to play without sight of the board, visualizing the position in his head and calling out his moves after due thought.

1 ...c5

The Sicilian Defence. Over 200 years later it remains one of the most popular of all openings.

2 f4 e6
3 Nf3 Nc6
4 c3 d5
5 e5 f5
6 d4

The opening has transposed to a French Defence. Already there is an obvious major difference in the style of play as compared to the Greco game. Both sides have used their pawns well and have created a definite structure involving pawn chains. White's plan is to continue his development and then use his extra space to help him launch an attack. Black's plan is to use the solid structure to keep his position safe from assault and, at the same time, he will try to break down the white structure. Philidor excelled in such positions.

6 ...Nh6

Good players don't develop their knights on the edge of the board without a sensible reason. This knight is heading for f7, from where it will defend his position and exert pressure on the e5 square.

7 a3 Nf7
8 Be3 Qb6

Novices are advised to keep their queens at home early in the game. In this type of position ...Qb6 is normal, as it applies pressure to the d- and b-pawns.

9 Qd2 Bd7
10 Qf2 c4

11 Bxc4

Sharp play from Atwood, who is clearly unwilling to allow Philidor to achieve one of his trademark pawn clamps on the queenside. Indeed, Black has to be careful here; White will win back the piece by force over the next couple of moves and Black must make sure his position can hold firm against the forthcoming tactics.

11 ...dxc4
12 d5

This is the point of Atwood's temporary bishop sacrifice. The twin threats of the discovered attack on Philidor's queen, together with the pawn attack on the knight, will need careful handling.

12 ...Qc7

A safe option. 12 ...Ncxe5!? is an interesting alternative. The knight is going to be captured anyway and taking one of the target pawns is a reasonable achievement. The point is that 13 Bxb6 allows the knight fork 13 ...Nd3+, instantly winning back the queen. Furthermore, 13 Nxe5 Nxe5 renews the threat and 13 fxe5 Qa5 leaves the white pawn centre under pressure, especially as 14 d6? loses a key pawn to 14 ...Nxe5.

13 dxc6 Bxc6
14 Bxa7 Bxf3

Forcing a weakness in the pawn structure, as 15 Qxf3 would lose the bishop (15 ...Rxa7).

15 gxf3 g5

Instantly exploiting the weakened pawns. The reflex action to ...g5 would normally be g2-g3, to meet ...gxf4 with gxf4, retaining pawn support of e5. Atwood no longer has that possibility.

16 Be3 gxf4
17 Bxf4 Nxe5
18 Bxe5 Qxe5+
19 Qe2 Qxe2+
20 Kxe2 h5
21 Nd2 Rc8
22 Rhg1 Kf7

Both sides are playing well but Philidor has a slight advantage. He has more space and his bishop has more potential than the white knight (which is struggling to find its way to an active square). Note how the bishop works so well with the black pawns; posted on white squares, they do not impede the bishop's mobility. If Philidor's bishop were placed on the white squares, then it would have more problems finding activity.

23 Rg2 Be7
24 Rag1 Bf6
25 Nf1 e5
26 Ne3 Ke6
27 Rd1 Rhg8
28 Rxg8 Rxg8
29 Nxc4

The knight has found activity but this move is possibly a mistake as it allows the black rook to penetrate to the seventh rank. 29 Kf1, to protect the g2 square, would have been an improvement.

29 ...Rg2+
30 Kd3 Rxh2

Philidor now has a passed h-pawn and he will hope to push it as soon as possible. Atwood has three pawns against one on the queenside - a very dangerous pawn majority - but he needs to start pushing them as quickly as possible if they are to make any impact on the game.

31 Rd2 Rh3
32 Ke2 b5

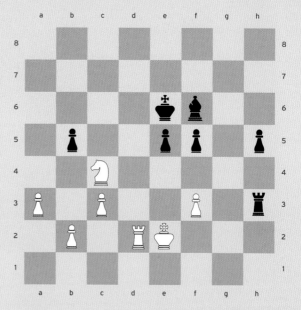

Another excellent pawn move from Philidor. He attacks the knight and makes it more difficult for White to advance the queenside pawns. If the knight sinks itself into d6 - protected by the rook - it is soon lost; 33 Nd6 Rh2+ 34 Kd1 Rxd2+ 35 Kxd2 Kxd6. Another faulty try is 33 Rd6+?? when, after the simple 33 ...Ke7, White suddenly loses a piece because if the knight moves away it leaves the rook unprotected.

33 Ne3 Rh2+
34 Ke1 Rxd2
35 Kxd2 Bg5

This pin ensures Philidor will be able to exchange the last minor pieces and produce a winning king and pawn ending.

36 Ke2 Bxe3
37 Kxe3

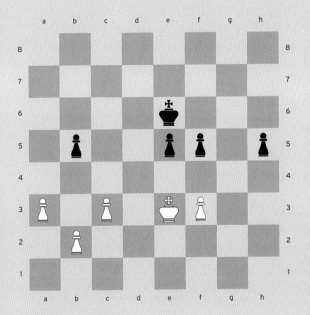

37 ...h4
38 Kf2 e4

Creating a second passed pawn, whether White plays 39 fxe4 (which will be met by 39 ...fxe4) or not. His king simply cannot stop both pawns at once.

39 Kg2 e3
40 Kh3 e2

Philidor is all set to acquire a new queen, so Atwood resigned here.

0-1

Players have handled their pawns much more responsibly since Philidor showed the world how important and useful they really are. There are occasional attempts to fly in the face of conventional wisdom, but these usually end in disaster. The following game shows how a strong player manages to punish an early avalanche of pawns.

Istvan Csom vs. Viktor Korchnoi
Asztalos Memorial, Gyula, 1965

1 d4 Nf6
2 c4 g6
3 d5

Korchnoi is a great expert in the Grunfeld Defence (3 Nc3 d5) and Csom clearly doesn't want to head into his opponent's specialist area. By playing d4-d5 so soon in the game, he is taking on a great responsibility. Black will be able to chip away at the centre from a very early stage.

3 ...Bg7
4 Nc3 0-0
5 e4 d6
6 Be2 c6

The first strike at the centre. It would be a mistake for White to play 7 dxc6; he has to try to maintain his pawn centre for as long as he possibly can. Black could reply with either 7 ...bxc6 (it's good to get more pawns in the centre) or 7 ...Nxc6 (to develop the knight to a very good square).

7 Be3 a6

Planning 8 ...b5 to attack the c-pawn.

8 a4

A standard response to 7 ...a6. If Black persists with 8 ...b5, he will lose a pawn as White outguns him on that square.

8 ...a5

A fine positional idea. The pawn moves for the second time in two moves. This would normally constitute a waste of a valuable move (or tempo) but the idea is to make sure that the b4 square is left firmly under Black's control. White can never attack or defend that square with a pawn and Black will use it as an outpost for a knight.

9 g4

An ambitious move. Csom is hoping to use his extra space as a basis for an attack. The danger is that if the attack fails to materialize, then he will be left with a lot of weaknesses and his king will never be able to find a safe haven.

9 ...Na6

Preparing to hop into b4.

10 f4

10 ...Nd7

Both knights are eyeing up the weakened squares on the queenside (b4 and c5). Korchnoi's king's bishop has also been unleashed and it is exerting considerable pressure all along the long diagonal.

11 h4

An extreme example of a pawn storm!

11 ...Ndc5
12 Bf3 Qb6
13 Qd2

13 ...Qxb2!

A wonderful move. Korchnoi sacrifices his queen, but it's only a temporary sacrifice. He will win the queen back with interest.

14 Qxb2 Nd3+

The knight fork guarantees Korchnoi a material advantage. White must lose his queen.

15 Kd2 Nxb2

Korchnoi is a pawn ahead and he is threatening to capture a second one, on c4.

16 Be2

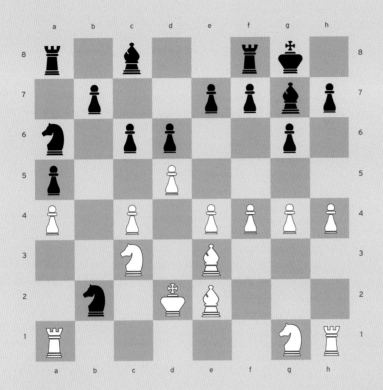

Csom protects the c-pawn and hopes to trap the knight on b2, which is short of exit squares. But Korchnoi has seen a little deeper into the position.

16 ...Bxg4!!
This must have been a shock for Csom. Korchnoi threatens to exchange the bishops with 17 ...Bxe2 and then play 18 ...Nxc4, leaving him with a winning material advantage. Csom can capture the bishop with 17 Bxg4 but after 17 ...Nxc4+ 18 Kd3 Nxe3 19 Kxe3 Bxc3 Korchnoi will be three pawns ahead and White's position would be hopeless. Csom resigned here.
0-1

Incidentally, Korchnoi was in terrific form in this tournament. He won 14 and drew one of his 15 games, taking first place, five and a half points clear of his nearest rivals.

Pawn weaknesses become more important in the endgame.

White to play

The pawns are equal in number but the quality of White's is far higher than his opponent's. White's plan is simple: to use the king to attack the black pawns, capture some of them and advance a pawn to the eighth rank to obtain a new queen. Black cannot hope to stop this plan because his pawns will be unable to defend each other.

Hero of Positional Play – Tigran Petrosian

Our positional hero was, like Mikhail Tal, a World Champion. He even beat the same player – Mikhail Botvinnik – to take the title, in 1963. However, their respective playing styles couldn't have been more different. While Tal was busy blowing away his shell-shocked opponents with devastating attacks, Tigran Petrosian was enjoying terrific success with his own brand of play.

With the nickname 'Iron Tigran', our positional hero specialized in outmanoeuvring his opponents over the course of lengthy games, in which he would very gradually gain control of the board, square by square, slowly squeezing the life from his victims.

Petrosian also possessed a very pronounced sense of danger and he was usually able to snuff out any potential trouble before it even got started, leaving his opponents demoralized and often unable to work out what they had done wrong on their way to defeat.

When Petrosian played his first match for the World Championship, he lost the first game and then recovered his composure with three draws before striking back in the fifth game.

Petrosian gained a very slight advantage from the earliest stages of the game and proceeded to nurse this tiny edge all the way to victory. This game set Petrosian back on course to take the title. Of the remaining games in the match he won four, drew 11 and lost only one.

As a rule in my games, when I have a choice between two continuations, one of which has unclear consequences (although instinct tells me that my chances will be more favourable), and the other leads to a clear and lasting advantage, I always prefer the clarity to complexity and risk.

PETROSIAN, IN SECOND PIATIGORSKY CUP

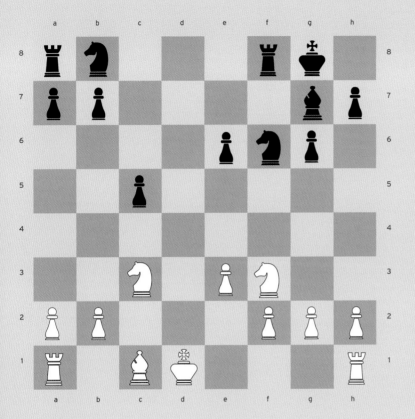

Tigran Petrosian vs. Mikhail Botvinnik
Game 5, World Championship Match, Moscow, 1963

1 c4 g6
2 d4 Nf6
3 Nc3 d5
4 Nf3 Bg7
5 e3 0-0
6 Be2 dxc4
7 Bxc4 c5
8 d5 e6
9 dxe6 Qxd1+
10 Kxd1 Bxe6
11 Bxe6 fxe6

The game has started very quietly and even the queens have been exchanged. Match commentators and spectators were predicting an early draw. However, Petrosian has created a weakness in Botvinnik's pawn structure; the pawn on e6 is isolated and potentially weak. The square in front of the pawn can be used as an outpost for White's pieces (especially the knights) because they cannot be chased away by enemy pawns.

Meanwhile, Black's queenside pawn majority could turn out to be an advantage for him deeper into the endgame. The idea is simple: if three pawns advance against two, then one may be able to force its way through to become a new queen.

12 Ke2 Nc6
13 Rd1 Rad8
14 Rxd8 Rxd8
15 Ng5 Re8
16 Nge4 Nxe4
17 Nxe4 b6
18 Rb1 Nb4
19 Bd2

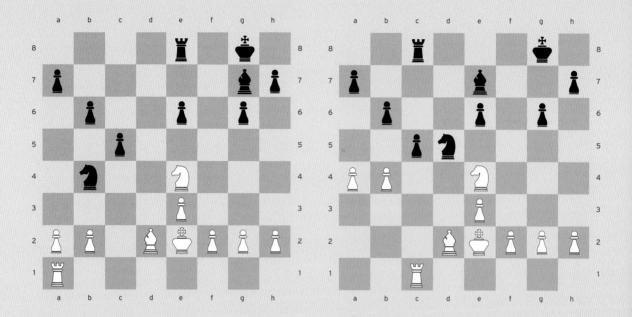

It looks like Black can win a pawn here with 19 ...Nxa2, which would leave him with an even bigger pawn majority on the queenside (three pawns vs. one) but White would reply with 20 Ra1 (*skewering* the knight against the a7-pawn) 20 ...Nb4 21 Bxb4 cxb4 22 Rxa7 Bxb2 23 Rb7 when both of Black's queenside pawns are weak and liable to be captured.

19 ...Nd5
20 a4 Rc8
21 b3 Bf8
22 Rc1 Be7
23 b4!

An excellent move by Petrosian, presenting Botvinnik with an unpleasant choice.

23 ...Nxb4? would be a blunder, allowing 23 Bxb4! as the c-pawn is pinned (23 ...cxb4 24 Rxc8).

23 ...Kf7 24 bxc5 bxc5 leaves Black with a second weak pawn which will come under serious attack from all of White's pieces. Instead, Botvinnik advances the pawn but it gets cut off from its colleagues.

23 ...c4
24 b5 Kf7
25 Bc3 Ba3
26 Rc2 Nxc3+
White was intending the sequence of moves, Nd2, g3 (to stop the black knight coming to f4) and e4, chasing away the knight and then winning the c4 pawn.

27 Rxc3 Bb4
28 Rc2 Ke7

29 Nd2 c3
30 Ne4 Ba5
31 Kd3

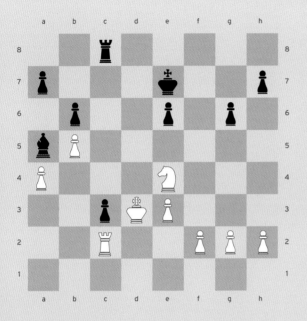

chance to keep the knight on the board and is happy to allow the h-pawn to be captured.

34 Ne4 Rxh2
35 Kd4

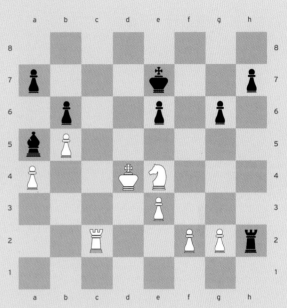

A passed pawn can be very dangerous in endgames but in this case Petrosian's acute sense of danger and positional mastery has enabled him to keep it firmly under lock and key. Note how active his king is, from now until the end of the game, and how he keeps his pieces on white squares so Botvinnik's bishop cannot attack them.

31 ...Rd8+
Botvinnik knows the c-pawn cannot be saved so he makes his rook more active in order to seek counterplay.

32 Kc4 Rd1
33 Nxc3 Rh1

Petrosian thought that Botvinnik should have played 33 ...Bxc3, with chances of saving the game, despite being a pawn down. The point is that the knight is a much better piece than the bishop in this position. Petrosian jumps at the

A simple comparison of the white and black pieces should be enough to show that White's advantage is reaching serious proportions. His king, rook and knight are all much more powerfully placed than their black counterparts. If Black gets greedy and captures another pawn with 36 ...Rxg2, it would end badly after 37 Rc7+ when his whole position would collapse. From now, until the end of the game, the white pieces gradually push forward and slowly squeeze the life out of the black position.

35 ...Kd7	**42 Re6 Bd8**
36 g3 Bb4	**43 Rd6+ Kc8**
37 Ke5 Rh5+	**44 Ke8 Bc7**
38 Kf6 Be7+	**45 Rc6 Rd1**
39 Kg7 e5	**46 Ng5 Rd8+**
40 Rc6 Rh1	**47 Kf7 Rd7+**
41 Kf7 Ra1	**48 Kg8**

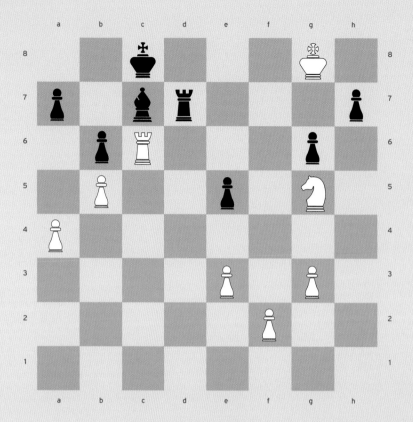

Black has been strangled and is now left without a single good move.

48 ...Kd8 49 Ne6+ Kc8 50 Rxc7+ Rxc7 51 Nxc7 Kxc7 52 Kxh7 allows White to mop up the pawns and eventually promote one of his own.

48 ...Rd8+ loses more pawns after simply 49 Kxh7.

48 ...Kb7 or 48 ...Kb8 both allow 49 Nxh7.

48 ...h5 temporarily saves the pawn, but loses the g-pawn after 49 Rxg6.

Black didn't fancy any of those options and decided to resign instead.

1-0

On playing through this game, one thing should be immediately apparent; Petrosian's best games, played in his finest positional style, would usually be much longer than Tal's tactical fireworks. The best Petrosian games are by no means less brilliant than Tal's, but they are instructive in quite different ways. Tal's best games will always be more popular in chess magazines and books because of their brevity but the keen student will learn just as much from Petrosian's positional crushes.

Petrosian excelled in the endgame. He was at his best when he had a solid advantage and his opponent was forced to defend, with little chance of counterplay. Petrosian would then be perfectly happy to manoeuvre, for as long as it took the opponent to crack under the sustained pressure. The following game is very long but it is a fine demonstration of Petrosian's patience and determination.

Tigran Petrosian vs. Bozidar Ivanovic
Bar, 1980

1 c4 e6
2 Nf3 d5
3 b3

Petrosian plays a quiet, positional opening and one which avoids long theoretical lines.

3 ...c5
4 e3 Nc6
5 cxd5 exd5
6 Bb2 Nf6
7 Bb5 Be7
8 0-0 0-0
9 d4 Bg4
10 dxc5 Bxc5

Petrosian has given his opponent an isolated queen's pawn and he will try to prove it is a weakness. Positional players pay much more attention to pawn structures than tactical players, because pawn weaknesses can often be exploited in the endgame. On the other hand, tacticians are more likely to achieve a decisive result by a middlegame attack.

11 Nc3 Rc8
12 Be2 Bd6
13 Rc1 Bb8
14 Re1 Re8
15 g3

This is an unusual move. Most players would prefer to leave their kingside pawns exactly as they were, but Petrosian feels that any potential weaknesses on the white squares can be easily managed. Black was probably going to play ...Qd6 soon, to threaten ...Bxf3 and ...Qxh2+,

but Petrosian had a habit of snuffing out his opponents' plans before they even got off the ground.

15 ...h5

Ivanovic rushes to attack on the kingside, hoping to use White's g-pawn as a lever to prise open a path to the king.

16 Na4 Qe7
17 Nh4 Ne5

Petrosian's knight moves to the side of the board look eccentric but he is entertaining ideas of occupying the c5 and f5 squares (after the bishops are exchanged). In reply, Ivanovic correctly centralizes his pieces. A period of manoeuvring follows, until Petrosian uncorks a couple of surprises on moves 23 and 24.

18 Rxc8 Rxc8
19 Nc3 Qb4
20 Qd4 a5
21 f3 Bh3
22 Rd1 Ba7

Ivanovic sets a trap. Petrosian could play it safe here with 23 Qd2, but he accepts the bait instead.

23 Qxe5 Re8

The white queen has no safe squares. Petrosian could swap his queen for the rook with 24 Qxe8+ Nxe8 but he has something stronger in mind.

24 Qxf6!

A wonderfully creative idea, sparking off a series of tactical blows.

24 ...gxf6
25 Nxd5 Rxe3

Black tries to retain the complications. If he simply moves his queen, he encounters problems. For example, 25 ...Qd6?? loses to 26 Nxf6+ and there's a discovered attack by the rook on the queen. 25 ...Qf8? allows 26 Nxf6+ Kh8 27 Nxe8+ Kh7 28 Nf6+ with a winning attack. The safest seems to be 25 ...Qc5, when after 26 Nxf6+ it isn't at all clear whether or not Black's king is safe, despite his material advantage.

26 Nxb4 Rxe2+
27 Bd4 Bxd4+
28 Rxd4 axb4
29 Rxb4 Rxa2
30 Rxb7 Kg7

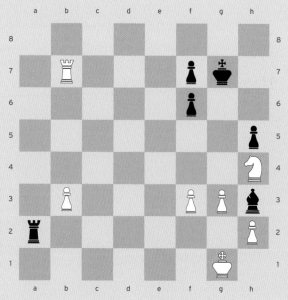

Incredibly, the great complications have calmed down to produce a normal-looking endgame. Petrosian has two advantages: an extra pawn on the queenside and the better pawn structure on the kingside. It is a difficult position to win and it will take a lot of time if Black defends well.

31 Rb5 Rb2
Step one: Exchange the b-pawn for the black h-pawn.

32 Rxh5 Rb1+
33 Kf2 Rb2+
34 Ke1 Rb1+
35 Kd2 Rxb3
36 g4 Bf1
37 Ke1
Step two: Improve the position of the king. It needs to support the white pawns as much as possible.

37 ...Ba6
38 Kf2 Bb7
39 Rc5 Kg8
40 Kg3
Step three: Try to induce a further weakening of the black pawns. This takes a few moves.

40 ...Kf8
41 Rf5 Kg7
42 Rf4 Bc8
43 Rc4 Be6
44 Rc5 Rd3
45 Rc2 Ra3
46 Rd2 Bc8
47 Rd8 Rc3
48 Re8 Kh6
49 Re7 f5

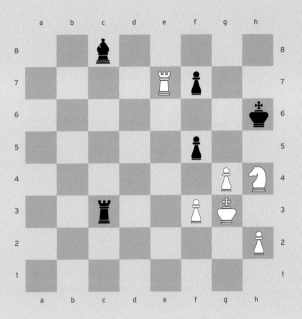

This is a sign that Ivanovic is losing patience. It is extremely difficult to defend a slightly inferior position and the automatic reaction is to try to do something active as soon as possible. However, he could still have tried sitting tight with 49 ...Be6 or 49 ...Kg7.

50 g5+ Kxg5
51 Rxf7
Step four: Advance the passed h-pawn. More manoeuvring is required.

51 ...Be6
52 Rg7+ Kf6
53 Ra7 Bd5
54 Ra6+ Bc6
55 Ra5 Bd7
56 Rd5 Be6
57 Rd2 Bf7
58 Ng2 Bh5
59 Rf2 Bf7
60 Nf4 Rc8
61 Rb2 Rc6
62 h4

The h-pawn is on its way at last, but it doesn't move again until move 113. Meanwhile, Petrosian proceeds to play his favourite game of cat and mouse. How much longer can the opponent endure the pressure before he cracks?

62 ...Ra6	75 Rd5 Kf6
63 Rb8 Rc6	76 Rd8 Ra6
64 Rh8 Kg7	77 Rh8 Kg7
65 Rd8 Kf6	78 Rh7+ Kg8
66 Nh3 Ke7	79 Rd7 Ra5
67 Rh8 Bd5	80 Kf4 Bc6
68 Rh7+ Kf6	81 Rc7 Be8
69 Nf4 Rc5	82 Ne6 Bh5
70 Rh6+ Kg7	83 Rg7+ Kh8
71 Rg6+ Kf7	84 Rd7 Ra6
72 Rd6 Ba8	85 Nd4 Ra3
73 Nh3 Rc6	86 Rb7 Ra4
74 Ng5+ Ke7	87 Ke5 Rxd4

Finally, Black has reached the point where he can no longer stand the pressure and seemingly endless manoeuvring. He thinks the bishop and pawn can protect each other to form a stronghold, but Petrosian eventually grinds him down.

88 Kxd4 Bxf3
89 Re7 f4

Giving up the f-pawn and bringing White's victory closer. However, if he had tried to sit tight with the bishop and pawn, the white king would simply penetrate Black's position on the dark squares by 90 Ke5, 91 Kf6, 92 Kg5, after which would follow the advance of the h-pawn.

90 Ke5 Bh5
91 Kxf4 Bg6
92 Kg5

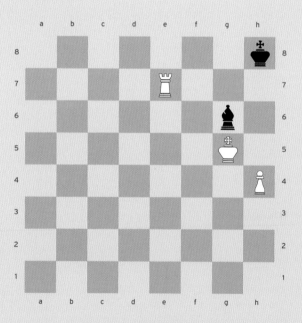

White is clearly winning and it only remains to continue step four of his original endgame plan - to push the h-pawn. Once again, Petrosian shows his immense patience and is not in the least concerned how long the game goes on.

92 ...Bh7	103 Kh5 Kf7
93 Kh6 Bg8	104 Rg1 Bd3
94 Rb7 Bc4	105 Rg5 Be2+
95 Rh7+ Kg8	106 Kh6 Bd3
96 Rc7 Bd3	107 Rg7+ Kf8
97 Rc8+ Kf7	108 Rg1 Bc2
98 Rc3 Be4	109 Rg3 Kf7
99 Rg3 Bc2	110 Kh5 Bd1+
100 Rg7+ Kf8	111 Kg5 Kg7
101 Rg2 Bd3	112 Rc3 Be2
102 Rg3 Bc2	

White's only technical problem is to avoid the danger of stalemate, which could arise right now if he plays his rook to f8, d8, c8, b8 or a8.

118 Re7 Bd5
119 h7 Be4+
120 Kh6 Bg6
121 Rd7 Be8
122 Rd6 Bd7
123 Rf6

Now the pawn moves – at last.

113 h5 Ba6
114 h6+ Kh8
115 Kg6 Bb7
116 Re3 Bd5
117 Re8+ Bg8

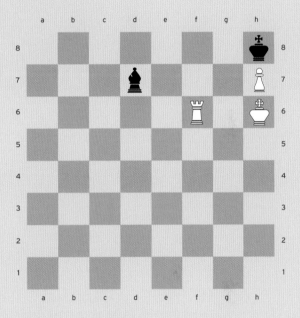

Black resigned, as checkmate is inevitable (123 ... Be6 124 Re8+ Bg8 125 Rxg8 checkmate).

1-0

WHEN HEROES MEET

What happened when Tal, the master of tactical play, had to play against Tigran Petrosian, the master of positional play? Could the strongest attack beat the toughest defence? In fact, Tal played Petrosian many times from the mid-1950s to the early 1980s. The vast majority of the encounters ended in draws and Petrosian had a slight edge in the number of wins they scored against each other.

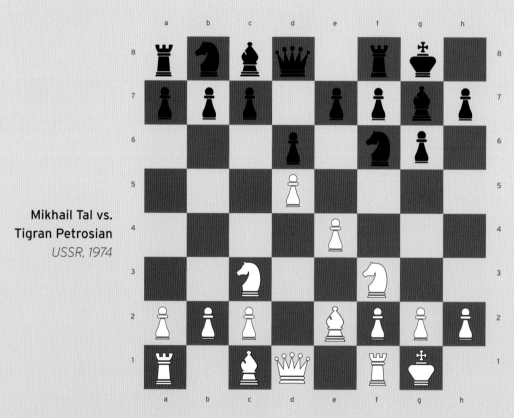

Mikhail Tal vs.
Tigran Petrosian
USSR, 1974

In the right sort of position Tal was unstoppable. This was his most devastating game against Petrosian.

1 e4 g6
2 d4 Bg7
The so-called Modern Defence. It is a surprising choice by Petrosian, who usually favoured the French or Caro-Kann Defences when he played Tal. White is invited to construct any sort of position he likes and Black's task will be to try to break it down.

3 Nc3 d6
4 Nf3 Nf6
5 Be2 0-0
6 0-0 Nc6
7 d5 Nb8
It looks odd for Black to develop his knight and allow it to be driven back immediately. The logic

behind the idea is that the knight will be able to relocate quickly to a central square, possibly at c5 (after ...Nbd7). White's d-pawn no longer controls the central black squares and Black has options of chipping away at the centre with ...c6 or ...e6.

8 Re1 e5
9 dxe6
The *en passant* capture prevents the position from becoming closed. Tal prefers to keep things as open and dynamic as possible.

9 ...Bxe6
10 Bf4 h6
This is a mistake as it weakens the king's position. Not a good idea against Tal. Petrosian should have developed his queen's knight.

11 Nd4 Bd7
12 Qd2 Kh7
13 e5 dxe5
14 Bxe5 Ne4
15 Nxe4 Bxe5
16 Nf3 Bg7
17 Rad1

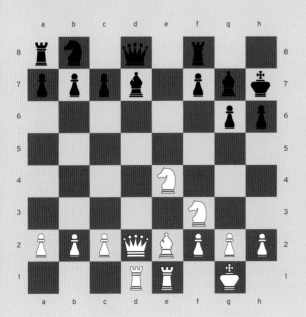

Tal's pieces are all excellently placed and ready for action. Petrosian's queenside pieces are still undeveloped and there are weaknesses around his king. This is the sort of position Tal always loved to play and it is no surprise that he finishes off the game quickly.

17 ...Qc8
18 Bc4 Be8

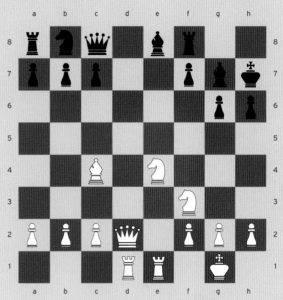

It's time for a typical Tal sacrifice.

19 Neg5+!
Petrosian has three choices. If he retreats his king with 19 ...Kg8 then Tal can sacrifice again with 20 Ne6!! which traps the black rook. 20 ...fxe6 21 Bxe6+ is not an acceptable solution to the problem as then Petrosian will lose his queen. 19 ...Kh8 is better, but still leads to serious trouble after 20 Ne6!!

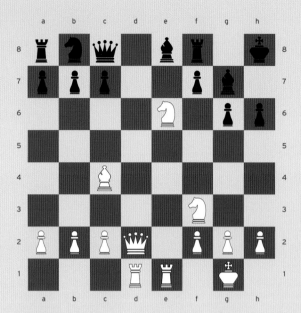

Analysis diagram

Play could continue 20 ...fxe6 21 Bxe6 when Black has to give up his extra material with 21 ...Bd7 22 Bxd7 Nxd7 23 Qxd7 and White has a large advantage. The only other option is the one played in the game – accepting the sacrifice and hoping for the best.

19 ... hxg5
20 Nxg5+ Kg8
21 Qf4

With the simple plan of checkmating the black king by 22 Qh4 and 23 Qh7.

21 ...Nd7

Trying to get the knight to f6 so it can defend the h7 square.

22 Rxd7! Bxd7
23 Bxf7+

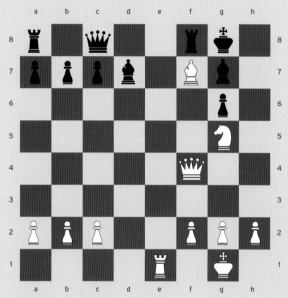

Analysis diagram

Total destruction. After 23 ...Rxf7 24 Qxf7+ Kh8 25 Qxg6 Bf5 Tal's knight performs a victory dance – 26 Nf7+ Kg8 27 Nh6+ Kh8 28 Nxf5 – to leave Petrosian three pawns down and with a defenceless king. Seeing this, Petrosian resigned.
1-0

The above game gives the strong impression that Tal could easily outplay Petrosian in a tactical situation. Yet Petrosian's tactical ability was also at a very high level and despite his preference for slow, manoeuvring games, he was more than capable of playing sharp positions when he had to.

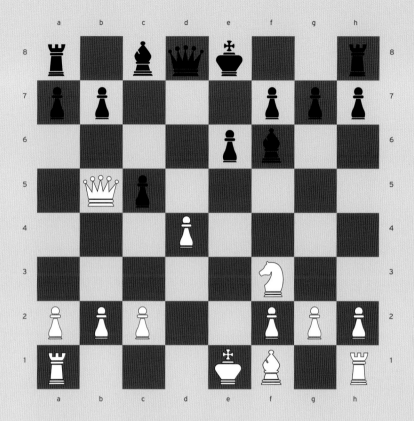

Mikhail Tal vs. Tigran Petrosian
Candidates Tournament, Curacao, 1962

1 e4 e6
2 d4 d5
The French Defence served Petrosian well throughout his career.

3 Nc3 Nf6
4 Bg5 dxe4
5 Nxe4 Nbd7
Petrosian is making a point of avoiding the sharpest lines in an effort to keep the position quiet. 3 ...Bb4 (Winawer Variation), 4 ...Bb4 (McCutcheon Variation) and 4 ...Be7 (Classical Variation) are all more combative ways to play.

6 Nxf6+ Nxf6
7 Nf3 c5
Petrosian would relish the chance to exchange queens should White play 8 dxc5. Tal naturally wants to keep the position lively but embarks on a faulty plan with his queen.

8 Qd3 Be7
9 Bxf6 Bxf6
10 Qb5+
This is the big idea. White will win a pawn (either on b7 or c5). However, Black obtains more than enough compensation in return.

10 ...Bd7
11 Qxb7

11 Qxc5 runs into 11 ...Rc8 when Black can take the initiative. For example, 12 Qxa7 Rxc2 and White is left with the inferior position. The black rook is in a very strong position and a further slip by White could be disastrous, e.g. 13 Qxb7? Qa5+ and it is doubtful whether the white king can survive.

11 ...Rb8
12 Qxa7 Rxb2
13 Bd3 cxd4
14 0-0 Bc6
15 Qa3 Qb6

For once, Tal's desire for tactical complications has backfired. Petrosian has outplayed him and has a strong grip on the position. His rook on b2 exerts a lot of pressure and it is not clear how Tal can chase it away. Black's two bishops are also very strong and control much of the board.

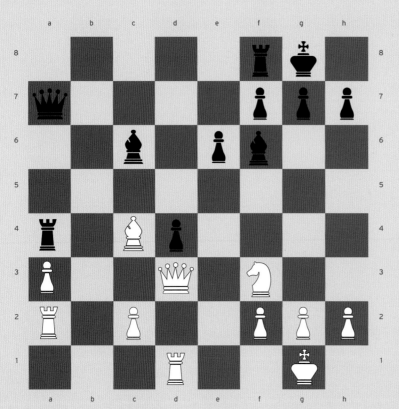

16 Bc4 Rb4
17 Qd3 0-0
18 a3 Ra4
19 Rfd1 Qa7
20 Ra2??

Tal is rushing to double his rooks (with 21 Rda1) in order to defend the weak a-pawn, but he has missed an elementary tactic.

Analysis diagram

20 ...Rxc4!

With the simple point that 21 Qxc4 fails to the skewer 21 ...Bd5 and 22 ...Bxa2, leaving Black with a decisive material advantage. Tal resigned.

0-1

Petrosian's Caro-Kann Defence held firm against Tal's tactics in another interesting encounter.

Mikhail Tal vs. Tigran Petrosian

USSR Championship, Moscow, 1973

1 e4 c6
2 d4 d5

In many ways, the Caro-Kann Defence is very similar to the French Defence. Black invites his opponent to construct a centre and will then set about undermining it.

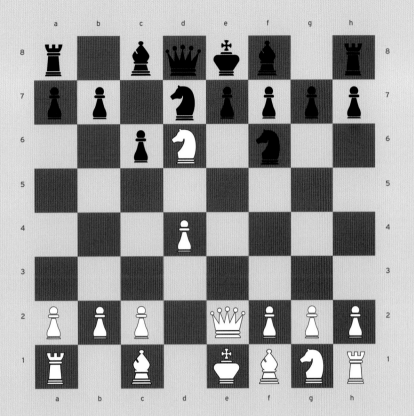

Analysis diagram

3 Nc3

Tal consistently played the committal Advance Variation (3 e5) in his 1961 World Championship match with Botvinnik, but it didn't really suit his style.

3 ...dxe4
4 Nxe4 Nd7

Other options are 4 ...Bf5 and 4 ...Nf6. Against the latter, White usually plays 5 Nxf6+ when Black has a choice of recaptures: 5 ... exf6 (solid) and 5 ...gxf6 (aggressive). 4 ...Nd7 prepares 5 ...Ngf6 so if White captures (6 Nxf6+) Black can reply with 6 ... Nxf6, keeping his pawn structure intact. White can set a devious trap here with 5 Qe2, intending to meet 5 ...Ngf6 with the stunning 6 Nd6 checkmate.

Unfortunately, if Black plays sensibly with 5 ...Ndf6, then White's queen just ends up in a poor place, where it blocks the development of his king's bishop.

5 Bc4 Ngf6
6 Ng5

Threatening an early checkmate with 7 Bxf7 but Black has a simple and solid defence.

6 ...e6
7 Qe2 Nb6
8 Bb3 a5
9 a4 h6
10 N5f3 c5
11 Bf4 Bd6
12 Be5 0-0
13 0-0-0

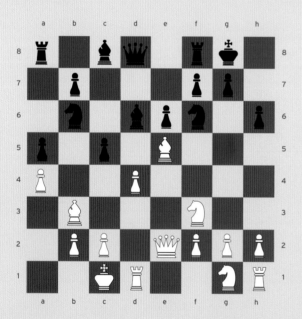

When players castle on opposite sides of the board they will immediately look for ways to attack each other's king. Both players have little gaps in their defensive walls. Black would prefer his h-pawn to be back on h7 and White would like his a-pawn to return to a2. Petrosian is quick to turn his attention to Tal's weakness.

13 ...c4!

Giving up his c-pawn to remove the guard of the a-pawn.

14 Bxc4 Nxa4
15 Nh3 Nb6
16 g4

It would be a mistake for Petrosian to capture the pawn with 16 ...Nxg4. Tal would reply with 17 Rhg1 and the rook on the open file will cause Black's king many problems.

16 ...a4

Both players are using their pawns as battering rams, intent on smashing their way through to the enemy king.

17 g5 hxg5
18 Nhxg5 a3
19 b3 Bb4
20 Rdg1 a2
21 Kb2 Nxc4+
22 Qxc4 Nd5
23 Ne4

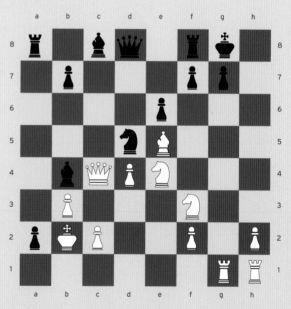

Storms are breaking over both kings. Before continuing with his own assault, Petrosian finds an excellent defensive resource to take the sting out of Tal's attack,

23 ...f6!

Forcing the bishop away and relieving some of the pressure on g7.

24 Bf4

Hoping for an exchange of pieces with 24 ...Nxf4 25 Qxb4, but Petrosian has something much stronger.

24 ...Ba3+
25 Ka1 Nxf4
26 h4 Rf7
27 Rg4 Qa5!

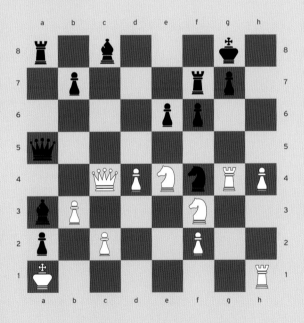

Tal is already a piece down and now he is faced with the deadly threat of 28 ...Bb2+! 29 Kxb2 a1=Q+ 30 Rxa1 Qxa1 checkmate. As there is no acceptable way to continue, he resigned.

0-1

Our final example of play between the two heroes sees Petrosian surprisingly trying to defeat Tal in sacrificial style, instead of waiting for his opponent's attack and then reacting accordingly.

Tigran Petrosian vs. Mikhail Tal
USSR Championship, Moscow, 1976

1 Nf3 Nf6
2 c4 c5
3 b3 e6
4 Bb2 Be7
5 e3 Nc6
6 d4 cxd4
7 exd4 d5
8 Bd3 b6
9 0-0 Bb7
10 Re1 Rc8
11 Nbd2 0-0
12 Rc1 Re8

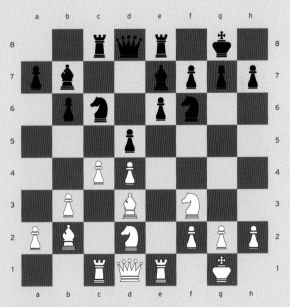

Nothing remarkable has happened so far. Both players have simply been content to develop their pieces.

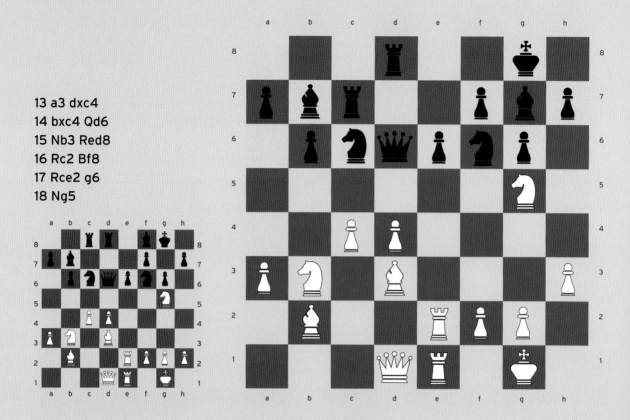

13 a3 dxc4
14 bxc4 Qd6
15 Nb3 Red8
16 Rc2 Bf8
17 Rce2 g6
18 Ng5

Petrosian rarely decentralized a piece without having a good idea in mind. Here he is limbering up for a Tal-like sacrifice.

18 ...Bg7
19 h3 Rc7
20 Qd2 would be a reasonable choice, waiting a little while longer before taking direct action. Petrosian decides to jump straight in.

20 Nxe6!?
An interesting idea. For the knight, White obtains two pawns and the initiative. However, Tal's position appears resilient and he has no poorly placed pieces.

22 ...fxe6
21 Rxe6 Qf8
22 d5 Nb8
23 Bc3 Na6
24 Nd4??

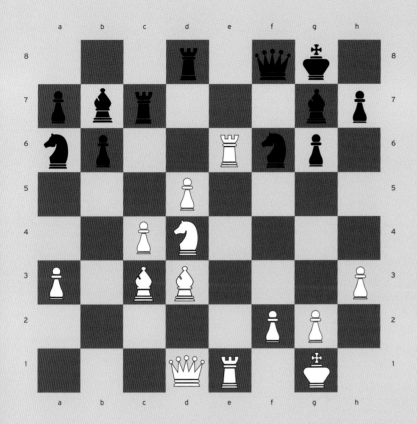

The idea is obvious. Petrosian would like to move his rook from e6 and replace it with his knight, where it would fork Tal's major pieces. Unfortunately 24 Nd4?? is actually a blunder, which Tal is quick to exploit. The undefended position of the bishop on c3 is the key to the refutation. Petrosian should have played 24 Qa1!, defending the bishop and increasing its power along the long diagonal.

24 ...Nxd5!

Tal was never going miss a shot like this. Although his knight can be captured it is not really a sacrifice because he obtains a bishop in return.

25 cxd5 Rxc3

White's position is in danger of a total collapse. The game does not last much longer.

26 Bxa6 Bxd5
27 Re7 Bf7
28 R7e4 Qc5

The terrible pin on the knight ensures Black will emerge a whole piece ahead, so White resigned.
0-1

HUMAN FACTORS

Chess games represent an unusual sporting contest. In other sports and games the result can be attributed to the strengths and brilliance of the opponent. A near-perfect serve in tennis is virtually impossible to return. A well-struck football, volleyed high into the back of the net, will have even the world's best goalkeeper clawing at thin air. A perfectly played snooker shot could send the cue ball all around the table and end up snookering the opponent, with a decisive gain in points.

In chess, there is only one person to blame for a defeat – and that is you. Both players start a game with the same number of pieces. Though White has the advantage of the first move, a perfectly played game should still end in a draw.

One player must make an error – or a series of errors – for an opponent to win. In most games, both players will make many small mistakes, even at the highest levels. A big mistake (blunder) should cost the game. The moves played on the board are solely the responsibility of the player. It makes sense to consider some of the factors leading to typical mistakes. Rather than blaming a defeat on bad luck, it would be more helpful to work out what went wrong and how an identical mistake can be avoided next time.

Nobody likes to lose but it is impossible to become a good chess player without suffering one's fair share of defeats. As chess is a mental game, defeats can get entrenched in a player's thoughts and give rise to negative feelings which can take some time to overcome. Even more so if the defeat comes in a game which has some special significance, such as a decisive battle in a school or club championship, a tough duel against a regular opponent or even a rare loss with a favourite opening. All these hurt, and so they should.

But every defeat should be regarded as a lesson and a step on the road to improvement. Any mistakes you made can be rectified before going into battle again. Did you lose with your favourite opening? Then study harder to see which move or plan was the culprit. Were you defeated by your main rival? Then adapt your way of playing and try to do better next time. Players who have a strong desire to improve their game will always do so. Those who are put off by painful defeats will rarely make significant advances.

The best way to improve is to keep studying and playing.

Procedure for Thinking

It is important to cultivate disciplined thinking when playing a game of chess. After every move the opponent makes, you should start off with the question – "What is my opponent trying to achieve with that move?" If your adversary is attacking one of your pieces, and the threat goes unnoticed, then that could be the end of the game. It is not an easy task to remain fully focused throughout the entire game (which could last three or more hours) but those who control their thought processes will have more success than those whose attention wavers.

If the opponent is threatening something, then you need to think to yourself:

1) How does the opponent's move affect my own plan?

2) What is the best way to deal with the threat?

If the opponent's move does not contain a direct threat, then it is useful to ensure that it does not spoil one's own intended plan. If it does, is there a way to deal with it – or is it necessary to devise a new plan?

Overlooking threats is the principal cause of defeat.

Mistakes and Blunders

A blunder is an extremely bad chess move. It usually changes the course of a game. A winning position can immediately be transformed into a loss as the result of a blunder. Every chess player will make blunders. Strong players will blunder less frequently than novices, but they too are not immune from this danger. Blunders can be very costly indeed, as the following example shows.

This was a very important World Championship game. A win for Chigorin would have levelled the match at 9-9 and he would have had every chance of going on to become the champion. He is a piece up and should play 32 Rxb7. Instead he played 32 Bb4?? which is a terrible blunder. Steinitz replied with 32 ...Rxh2+ and Chigorin resigned (0-1). Unfortunately for him, the only alternative to resigning is to play 33 Kg1 whereupon Steinitz would play 33 ... Rdg2 checkmate.

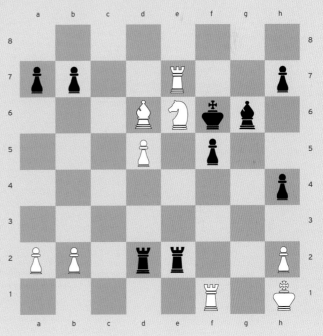

Mikhail Chigorin vs.
Wilhelm Steinitz
World Championship Match,
Havana, 1892
White to play

Chigorin remained one of the strongest players in the world but he never did become World Champion. His fatal blunder must have been extremely painful but at least he was in good company; all chess players, no matter how strong they may be, will blunder at some point.

There are numerous factors that might cause a blunder. These include:

1) *Tiredness*. It is not easy to concentrate for long periods of time and fatigue can take a hold.

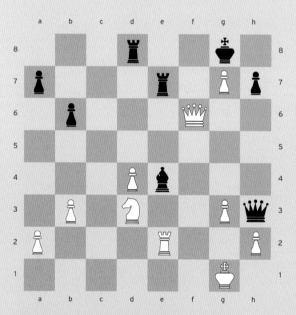

Viktor Korchnoi vs. Bob Wade
Capablanca Memorial, Cuba, 1963

The author of the original *The Batsford Book of Chess* should definitely have won this game against one of the world's strongest players. He is a rook up (though Korchnoi has three pawns for the rook, they don't look too dangerous). Korchnoi's king is also in danger. Yet White went on to win this game.

32 ... Qe6
Any fair exchange would suit Black. Korchnoi must keep the queens on the board to have any chance of fighting back.

33 Qf4 Rde8
33 ...Kxg7 is a good alternative, preventing the white g-pawn from making any impact on the game. The black king is safe enough after 34 Qg5+ Kh8.

34 Ne5 Bg6??
This throws away the advantage. Virtually any other sensible bishop move is better, with the centralizing 34 ...Bd5 probably the pick of the bunch. White's knight would be left pinned against his rook, but after 34 ...Bg6?? Korchnoi spots a cunning resource.

35 Nxg6!

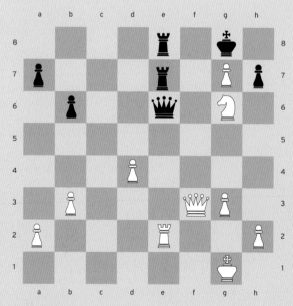

35 ...hxg6
The line 35 ...Qxe2 36 Qf8+! Rxf8 37 gxf8=Q checkmate demonstrates the danger with which Black is suddenly faced. Now he has to give up his queen for White's rook.

36 Rxe6 Rxe6
37 Kg2 Kxg7

In return for Wade's pair of rooks, Korchnoi has a queen and two extra pawns, with the d-pawn being particularly dangerous, as it is 'passed'. He duly won on move 63.

How did Bob Wade fail to win this game when he was a rook ahead? Twenty-five years later, I had the opportunity to ask him that question. "Sheer fatigue!" he replied. "I had been up most of the previous night reading Robert Travers' *Anatomy of a Murder!*"

2) *Nervousness.* It is good to feel a little nervous during a game, as it shows you are alert and ready for a fight. However, if the game has a particular sporting significance then excessive nervousness can be a problem. Imagine a situation where you are up against your greatest rival, or playing a key game in a match or tournament. Under these circumstances it is not so easy to escape the feeling of increased tension. The only way to overcome problems with nerves is through experience. The more crucial games you play – for example, those in which a title is at stake – the better you will be able to cope with the debilitating effects of nervous tension.

3) *Relaxation.* If the position is relatively quiet then it is easy to be lulled into a false sense of security and a reduction in your level of concentration. Relaxing in strong positions is also a common problem. Dropping your guard for just a single move might allow a resourceful player to fight back.

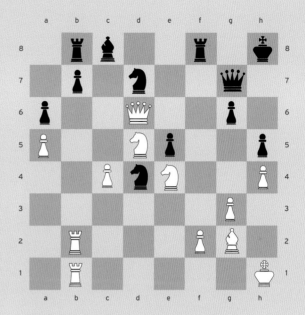

Tigran Petrosian vs. David Bronstein
Candidates Tournament, Amsterdam, 1956
Black to play

Here, Petrosian has a superb game. His pieces are wonderfully placed and Black can hardly move any of his men without suffering severe consequences. This is exactly the sort of position in which it is easy for the player who is control to relax prematurely and miss something simple. Bronstein played **35 ...Nf5** which obviously attacks Petrosian's queen. However, the great master of positional play, who would normally sense even a hint of trouble, missed the threat completely and played **36 Ng5??** allowing the simple **36 ...Nxd6**. White resigned. **0-1**.

4) *Miscalculation.* A short line of analysis – looking just one or two moves ahead – is fairly simple. The longer the analytical line, the more chance there is of missing something important. There is the same danger when the position is extremely complicated, as in the next example.

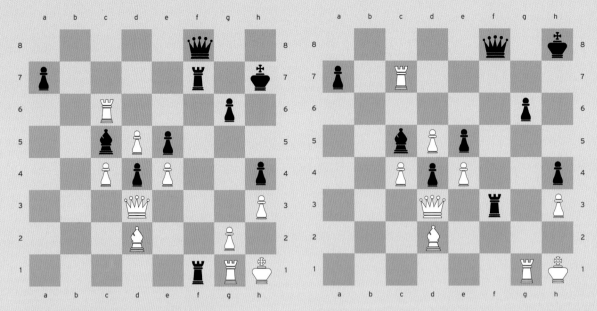

Anatoly Karpov vs. Garry Kasparov

Game 23, World Championship Match,
Seville, 1987
Black to play

This was a game in which Garry Kasparov
nearly lost his title of World Champion due to
a miscalculation. 50 ...Bb4 is probably the best
move, which may lead to a draw with best play.
Instead of that, Kasparov miscalculated badly. He
played:

50 ...R7f3??
51 gxf3 Rxf3
52 Rc7+ Kh8

Black's idea is now clear: his rook is attacking the
white queen and h-pawn. If the queen moves
away – for example, with 53 Qb1 – then 53 ...
Rxh3+ 54 Kg2 Qf3 is checkmate. Unfortunately
for Kasparov, Karpov found something much
stronger.

53 Bh6!
A counterattack on the black queen. Kasparov
has nothing better than to allow a trade of
queens, after which his attacking potential is
reduced virtually to zero.

53 ...Rxd3
54 Bxf8 Rxh3+
55 Kg2 Rg3+
56 Kh2 Rxg1
57 Bxc5 d3
Kasparov resigned here – **1-0** – because he
realized his position was absolutely hopeless
after 58Be3!, when the bishop can happily
sacrifice itself for the black d-pawn, safe in the
knowledge that his own passed c- and d-pawns
will sail down the board to promotion.

Next time you blunder, remember that even World Champions are vulnerable to making ridiculously bad moves, as demonstrated by the following selection of positions.

Larry Christiansen vs. Anatoly Karpov
Wijk aan Zee, 1993

1 d4 Nf6
2 c4 e6
3 Nf3 b6
4 a3 Ba6
5 Qc2 Bb7
6 Nc3 c5
7 e4 cxd4
8 Nxd4 Nc6
9 Nxc6 Bxc6
10 Bf4 Nh5
11 Be3 Bd6

Anatoly Karpov has won more chess tournaments than any other player in the history of chess. Yet here he has just played a very bad move, allowing Christiansen a winning tactic. Can you see White's best move?

12 Qd1
A clever move, forking two stray black pieces – the bishop on d6 and the knight on h5. Karpov resigned.
1-0

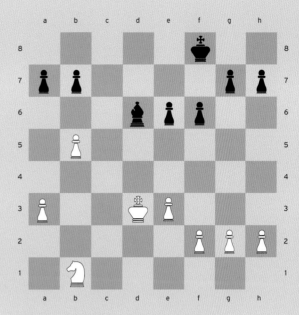

Boris Spassky vs. Bobby Fischer
Game 1, World Championship Match,
Reykjavik, 1972
Black to play

This position, just before Black's 29th move, was reached in the first game of the most famous match ever played for the World Championship. The game is heading for a draw, but Fischer wanted more and captured a pawn with **29 ... Bxh2??** What is wrong with this move?

Spassky played **30 g3!**, a standard way of trapping a greedy bishop. Fischer must have thought he could rescue the bishop after **30 ... h5** but he missed something. After **31 Ke2 h4 32 Kf3 h3 33 Kg4 Bg1 34 Kxh3** it looks as if the bishop can slip out of the trap with **34 ...Bxf2** but then **35 Bd2!** ensures it will soon be captured. Fischer tried **32 ...Ke7** instead but he couldn't save the bishop or the game (1-0, 56).

Fritz Saemisch vs. José Raul Capablanca
Karlsbad, 1929
Black to play

Of all the World Champions, Capablanca was one of toughest to beat. In this position he played a developing move that looked perfectly natural. **9 ...Ba6??** However, it is a major blunder. What should White play?

10 Qa4! pinning the knight and attacking the bishop. **10 ...Bb7** saves the bishop and protects the knight but then **11 d5!** wins the knight after all. (1-0, 62).

Time Pressure

Having to deal with a shortage of time can be a problem in games where you are using chess clocks. You might have thought for too long at certain moments in the game and left yourself too little time to complete your remaining moves. In this situation, it is essential to speed up as you approach the time control, in order to avoid losing on time. Of course, the accuracy of your moves can dip alarmingly in the rush to make the last few moves.

Typical mistakes in time-trouble include:
1) Trying to force the game tactically
2) Trying to simplify the position
3) Playing moves that are too committal - usually pawn moves.

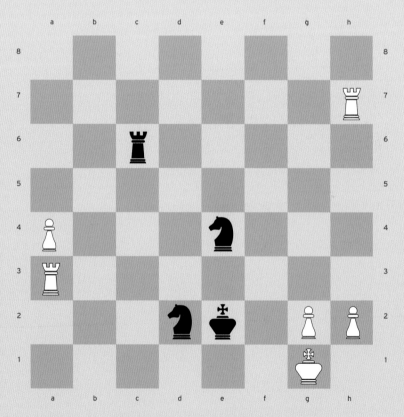

Viktor Korchnoi vs. Anatoly Karpov
Game 17, World Championship Match,
Baguio, 1978
White to play

The games of Viktor Korchnoi are full of fighting chess. However, playing for a win at every opportunity comes at a price: Korchnoi frequently left himself very short of time and had to rush his moves at critical moments. Inevitably, at times like this, there was sometimes a drop in the quality of his play. He should have won game 17 of his 1978 World Championship match, but a lack of thinking time, in conjunction with Karpov's expert defence, led to him frittering away most of his advantage.

In the position shown in the diagram, Korchnoi underestimated Black's potential threats and he played 39 Ra1?? He had to defend against 39 ...Rc1 checkmate but the best way to do it was to provide an escape square for the king with 39 g3! Unfortunately, after the move played, he walked into an alternative checkmate with 39 ... Nf3+! and had to resign the game immediately. After 40 Kh1 Nf2 is checkmate and 40 gxf3 Rg6+ 41 Kh1 Nf2+ is just as bad.
0-1

Checkmate!

This wasn't the only game in the match that Korchnoi lost because of a lack of thinking time at critical moments. When one considers he lost the match 5-6 (with an additional 21 draws) it can be appreciated how great a role time-trouble played in the contest.

The simplest way to avoid the perils of time pressure is to avoid it altogether. Easier said than done, of course. You have to establish a rhythm of play and avoid the temptation to analyze every variation to exhaustion.

Seeing Ahead

"How many moves can you see ahead?" is one of the most common questions asked by non-chessplayers. Of course, it is impossible to answer with a simple number. "It depends on the position" is the simplest reply. Sometimes one move is enough; sometimes, in very complicated positions, much deeper calculation is required, often branching out in various directions.

Ossip Bernstein vs. José Raul Capablanca
Moscow, 1914

This is a classic example of a player seeing just a little further than his opponent. Capablanca has a passed c-pawn and has been carefully advancing it down the board. Bernstein has done well to keep the c2 square heavily protected, thus preventing the pawn from advancing even further. Capablanca needs to move his rook, which is attacked by the knight, and he selected a move that set a trap.

25 ...Rc7
26 Nb5

Walking into the trap. If Bernstein had seen what was coming he would have secured his back rank by playing 26 h3! Instead he assumed Capablanca had simply blundered his c-pawn to a knight fork.

26 ...Rc5
27 Nxc3

It wasn't too late to keep his position safe with 27 Nd4 but Bernstein is still oblivious to the danger.

27 ...Nxc3
28 Rxc3 Rxc3
29 Rxc3 Qb2!!

A brilliant queen sacrifice that leaves White in a hopeless position. For example:

30 Qxb2 Rd1 checkmate.
30 Qf1 Qxc3 leaves Black a rook ahead.
30 Qe1 Qxc3! when 31 Qxc3 Rd1 32 Qe1 Rxe1 is checkmate.
30 Rc2 Qb1+ 31 Qf1 Qxc2 and Black is a rook ahead again. Bernstein resigned here. **0-1**

Age

It has often been said that "chess is a young person's game." This is because it takes an enormous amount of energy to compete successfully at a very high level. Stamina plays a major role in a chess player's success. It is not easy to keep on playing consistently strong moves after thinking deeply for four, five or six hours, and tiredness will increase the probability of blunders occurring on the board.

However, for novices, juniors and club players, age is largely irrelevant. Indeed, it's another factor that makes chess such an unusual and very accessible game. A person, aged 80, playing tennis with someone 60 or more years their junior, wouldn't have much hope of success, but on the chess board the physical difference will not be so important.

For some time it was reckoned that top chess players achieved peak performance at thirty years of age, when they enjoyed a healthy combination of maximum experience and maximum energy. Though this theory seems perfectly reasonable, there are many examples of older Grandmasters retaining their chess strength long after they have passed through the 30 barrier. In 1961, Mikhail Botvinnik, at the age of 50, surprised the chess world by winning a return match for the World Championship against Mikhail Tal, 25 years his junior. Tal had crushed Botvinnik in their first match, just one year earlier, and it was generally expected that he would do the same again. However, Botvinnik prepared thoroughly, in order to find ways to combat Tal's highly tactical play, and he won back his title in very convincing fashion. There are plenty of other examples. Viktor Korchnoi continued to play into his 80s and never lost his ferocious will to win. Similarly, Vassily Smyslov, World Champion back in 1957, came within one match victory of qualifying for a world title match in the 1980s. Two of his games

from his Candidates match against Zoltan Ribli are fabulous examples of an older man defeating a much younger opponent. Smyslov was 62 at the time of the match, whereas Ribli was only 32.

Vassily Smyslov vs. Zoltan Ribli
Game 5, Candidates Match, London, 1983

This is the fifth game of the match, which was tied at 2-2 at this point.

1 d4 Nf6
2 Nf3 e6
3 c4 d5
White has played a Queen's Gambit...

4 Nc3 c5
5 cxd5 Nxd5
...against which Black defends with the Semi-Tarrasch Defence.

6 e3 Nc6
7 Bd3 Be7
8 0-0 0-0
9 a3 cxd4
10 exd4 Bf6

The game is unbalanced and the positions of each side have both pluses and minuses. White has an isolated queen's pawn (commonly known as an IQP). This pawn could end up in trouble as it cannot be defended by another pawn. However, in return for the potential weakness, White enjoys more space for his pieces and has a foothold in the centre (the d4-pawn attacks the c5 and e5 squares). White's task is to use the extra space to prepare an attack against the black king. On the other hand, Black's position is solid and he has a ready-made plan of exerting significant pressure on the d4-pawn. He already has a knight and a bishop attacking it, but has less space than White and consequently his pieces are a little cramped. Also he needs to find a good way to develop his queen's bishop.

11 Qc2 h6

Ribli had to stop 12 Bxh7+ and he was reluctant to play 11 ... g6 due to 12 Bh6, exploiting the weakness on the black squares around his king. But now, after 11 ...h6, he will have to be very careful about the white squares in this same region.

12 Rd1 Qb6

Black needs more pieces to attack the d4-pawn. 12 ...Nxd4 13 Nxd4 Bxd4 14 Bh7+ Kh8 wins the pawn but loses a piece to 15 Rxd4.

13 Bc4 Rd8
14 Ne2 Bd7
15 Qe4 Nce7
16 Bd3 Ba4

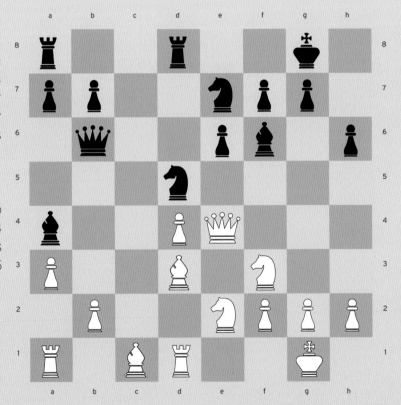

Ribli is playing riskily. It is extremely unusual to allow an attacking queen into the castled position, but Black hopes it will end up out of play once his knight goes to g6. 16 ...Ng6 was a safer option, blocking the queen's path to h7. 16 ...Bb5 was another good alternative. Exchanges tend to favour the side battling against an IQP because each time they bring him one step closer to the endgame, where the weakness of the pawn will be a marked disadvantage.

17 Qh7+ Kf8
18 Re1 Bb5

The right idea. White would prefer to keep his white-squared bishop on the board but if he retreats it, then Black could play 19 ...Bxe2, removing a key defender of the d4-pawn.

19 Bxb5 Qxb5
20 Ng3 Ng6
21 Ne5 Nde7

This is what Ribli had in mind. If he can keep the white queen trapped in the corner and out of the game, then his own queen will lay claim to being the most powerful piece on the board. Unfortunately for him, Smyslov has seen much deeper into the position and he now sacrifices his bishop to start a brilliant attack.

22 Bxh6!

Now 22 ...gxh6 would allow 23 Qxf7 checkmate.

22 ... Nxe5
23 Nh5 Nf3+

Black gives back his extra knight to split up the white kingside pawns.

24 gxf3 Nf5
25 Nxf6 Nxh6
26 d5 Qxb2

It looks like Black will give as good as he gets, but Smyslov has prepared a fantastic tactical sequence.

27 Qh8+ Ke7

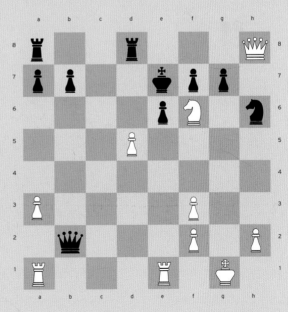

28 Rxe6+ fxe6
29 Qxg7+ Nf7
30 d6+ Rxd6

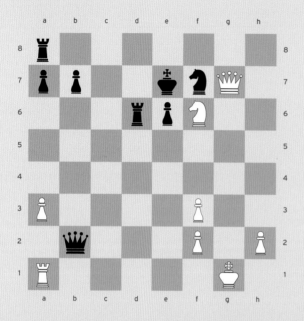

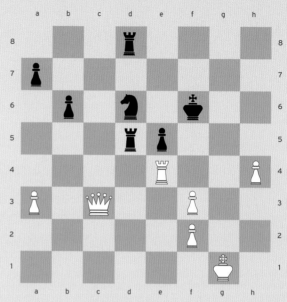

Why has Smyslov sacrificed so much material? His next move reveals his ultimate intention.

31 Nd5+

This is what he had spotted several moves ago. After this knight sacrifice, the white queen is magically able to capture the black queen.

31 ...Rxd5
32 Qxb2 b6

White's material advantage is decisive. Ribli plays on for a few more moves before resigning.

33 Qb4+ Kf6
34 Re1 Rh8
35 h4 Rhd8
36 Re4 Nd6
37 Qc3+ e5

Yet another sacrifice, but this one is only temporary as Smyslov quickly wins back the rook, thanks to the pin.

38 Rxe5 Rxe5
39 f4

Attacking a pinned piece is an important tactical idea. The rook cannot move away and so it will be captured by the pawn.

39 ...Nf7
40 fxe5+ Ke6

He can't even capture the pawn with 40 ...Nxe5, because 41 f4 would then repeat the same trick from move 39.

41 Qc4+

Black is helpless to prevent the advance of the white pawns, so Ribli resigned.
1-0

The seventh game of the match effectively sealed Smyslov's overall victory.

Vassily Smyslov vs. Zoltan Ribli
Game 7, Candidates Match, London 1983

1 d4 Nf6
2 Nf3 e6
3 c4 d5
4 Nc3 c5
5 cxd5 Nxd5
6 e3 Nc6
7 Bd3 Be7
8 0-0 0-0
9 a3 cxd4
10 exd4 Bf6

This is the same position they reached in game 5 of the match. It is common for players to continue to repeat the same openings during a match. Between games they will both try to find improvements on their previous play. On this occasion, it is Smyslov who is the first to vary.

11 Be4 Nce7
12 Ne5 g6
13 Bh6 Bg7
14 Bxg7 Kxg7
15 Rc1 b6
16 Nxd5 Nxd5

Smyslov's new plan is outwardly simple. His rook controls the open c-file and he wants to use it to invade the black position. Ribli is two moves from safety. He needs to develop his bishop and contest the open file with ...Rc8. Meanwhile his knight is defending the important c7 square, so Smyslov swaps it off.

17 Bxd5 Qxd5
Ribli hopes to complete his development and then attack the isolated queen's pawn. That is why he didn't play 17 ...exd5, which would not only leave him with an isolated pawn but also put an end to any attack he had planned along the d-file. However, that may have the better of the two options, as he now has to cope with Smyslov's rook entering his position.

18 Rc7 Bb7
Finally developing the bishop and threatening checkmate with 19 ...Qxg2.

19 Qg4 Rad8

Attacking the d-pawn again. Although Smyslov defends it with his next move, this was not necessary just yet. If, for example, he continued with 20 Rfc1, to double the rooks on the open file (usually a very strong idea), then Black would be unable to safely capture the pawn, as after 20 ...Qxd4 21 Qxd4 Rxd4 the bishop is left unprotected and White could just play 22 Rxb7.

20 Rd1 a5
21 h4

Black has to keep cool here. 21 ...h5, blocking the advance of the attacking h-pawn and striking the queen, looks tempting but loses quickly to 22 Qxg6+. The f7-pawn is pinned by the rook so the queen is safe.

21 ...Rc8
22 Rd7 Qe4
23 Qg5 Bc6
24 f3 Qf5

Ribli is defending well under pressure. 24 ...Qe2 was another tempting move but Smyslov had prepared a rook sacrifice with 25 Ng4 Qxd1+ 26 Kg2 and, despite having the move, Black is powerless to protect his king against the threats of 27 Qf6+ followed by 28 Nh6 checkmate and the similar 27 Qh6+ with 28 Nf6 checkmate.

25 Ra7 Ba4

Black could have exchanged the queens here with 25 ...Qxg5. When under attack, it is a good policy to swap off the opponent's most dangerous pieces. But here he comes up with the alternative plan of invading on the c-file and establishing a rook on the seventh rank.

26 Re1 Rc2
27 b4 Bb3
28 bxa5 bxa5
29 Re4 h6

Ribli should definitely have exchanged the queens here.

30 Qe3 Rb2
31 Rg4

Threatening 32 Rxg6+, exploiting the pin on the f-pawn by the rook on a7. White's attack is increasing in strength and Black is forced to weaken his kingside.

31 ...g5
32 hxg5 h5

A clever idea. Instead of the obvious recapture, Ribli tries hard to keep as many lines closed around his king as he can.

33 Rg3 h4
34 Rg4 h3
35 g6

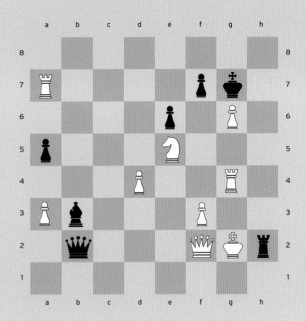

Yet again exploiting the pin on the f-pawn. Black's position is on the point of collapse. He tries one last desperate counter attack.

35 ...h2+
36 Kxh2 Rh8+
37 Kg3 Rxg2+
38 Kxg2 Qc2+
39 Qf2 Rh2+

Winning the white queen, but at a terrible cost. Black's only realistic hope is to force a draw by a perpetual check.

40 Kxh2 Qxf2+
41 Kh3 Qf1+
42 Rg2 Qh1+

White's king can indeed escape perpetual check, but he has to go for a walk to do so. After 43 Rh2 Qf1+ 44 Kh4 Qe1+ 45 Kh5, Black has run out of checks and White is ready to crash through the last remaining obstacle with 46 Rxf7+. So Ribli resigned.

1-0

For Smyslov to play so energetically in very complicated positions, against an opponent 30 years his junior, represents a remarkable achievement.

NON-HUMAN FACTORS

It's hard to recall a time when computers weren't an integral part of our lives, and the rise of the machines has had a massive impact on chess too.

During the 1980s and 1990s there were several challenge matches between the top Grandmasters and the best chess computers. The humans retained the edge for some time, but the programs gradually got stronger and started to notch up some very notable victories. Three high profile Man v Machine games featured none less than the World Champion of the time, Garry Kasparov. In 1994 he was knocked out of a PCA Rapidplay tournament by the Pentium 'ChessGenius' program.

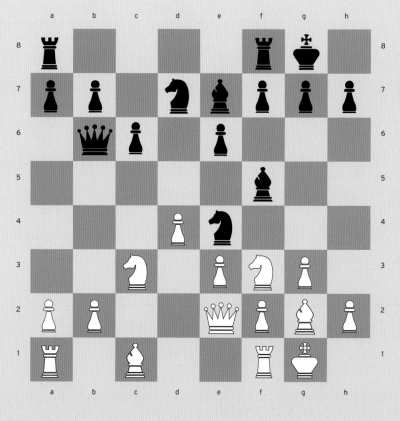

Garry Kasparov vs. Pentium Genius
PCA/Intel Grand Prix, London, 1994

1 c4 c6
2 d4 d5
3 Nf3 Nf6
4 Qc2 dxc4
5 Qxc4 Bf5
6 Nc3 Nbd7
7 g3 e6
8 Bg2 Be7
9 0-0 0-0
10 e3 Ne4
11 Qe2 Qb6

Kasparov keeps everything as safe and sound as possible. Computers excel at tactics and even back in 1994 they were more than a match for humans in that department. However, there were still ways to beat the computers positionally, as they struggled to appreciate and correctly assess long-term strategical plans. Indeed, nothing much of note happens for another 16 moves, as Kasparov is content simply to improve his position little by little.

12 Rd1 Rad8	20 Nc2 Qb6
13 Ne1 Ndf6	21 Bf4 c5
14 Nxe4 Nxe4	22 Be3 cxd4
15 f3 Nd6	23 Nxd4 Bc5
16 a4 Qb3	24 Rad1 e5
17 e4 Bg6	25 Nc2 Rxd3
18 Rd3 Qb4	26 Qxd3 Ne7
19 b3 Nc8	

Kasparov now decides to force the pace.

27 b4 Bxe3+
28 Qxe3 Rd8!

If 28 ...Qxe3+ 29 Nxe3, Kasparov's position would improve dramatically. His rook would be able to occupy the seventh rank (Rd7!) and his knight would be well placed to hop into d5. His problem now is that 29 Qxb6?? allows Black to win a rook (and the game) by playing 29 ...Rxd1+! before recapturing the queen with 30 ...axb6.

29 Rxd8+ Qxd8
30 Bf1 b6
31 Qc3 f6
32 Bc4+ Bf7
33 Ne3 Qd4!

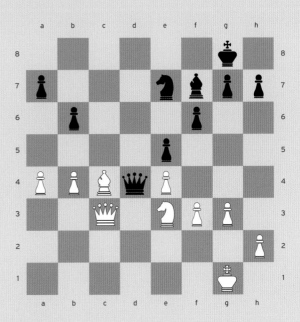

The game is heading for a draw.

34 Bxf7+ Kxf7

The question is – should Kasparov now exchange the queens? 35 Qxd4 exd4 gives Black a passed pawn, but one which is isolated. Against a human opponent he may well have opted to do this, but when playing computers there is a strong tendency to trust them when it comes to calculation of variations. Would the machine have allowed this continuation, if the pawn wasn't going to be strong? Kasparov trusts its judgement and keeps the queens on the board. Unfortunately, this decision proves to be his undoing.

35 Qb3+?! Kf8
36 Kg2 Qd2+
37 Kh3 Qe2
38 Ng2 h5
39 Qe3

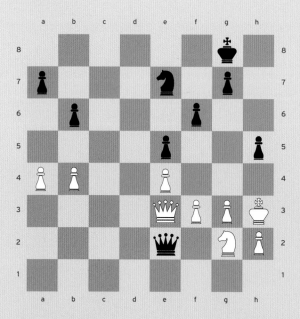

Kasparov changes his mind about exchanging queens, but this time the computer declines the offer. The white king has major problems, but these would instantly disappear with the departure of the queens.

39 ...Qc4!
40 Qd2 Qe6+
41 g4
The defence starts to crumble, but 41 Kh4? g5+ 42 Kxh5 Qh3+ was an even worse choice.

42 ...hxg4+
42 fxg4 Qc4
43 Qe1 Qb3+
44 Ne3 Qd3!
44 ...Qxa4 was perfectly good too, but the computer has spotted that the e-pawn cannot be defended and it understands that central pawns are usually more important than flank pawns. Indeed, the moves by the black queen have been particularly impressive throughout this game.

45 Kg3 Qxe4
46 Qd2 Qf4+
47 Kg2 Qd4

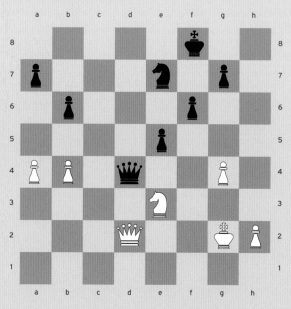

How ironic! The queens end up being exchanged on the same square as they should have been earlier. The position is now resignable but Kasparov plays on for a while, perhaps out of anger and frustration. He knows that embarrassing headlines will result from his defeat and so tries to delay the inevitable final outcome.

48 Qxd4 exd4
49 Nc4 Nc6
50 b5 Ne5
51 Nd6 d3
52 Kf2 Nxg4+
53 Ke1 Nxh2
54 Kd2 Nf3+
55 Kxd3 Ke7
56 Nf5+ Kf7
57 Ke4 Nd2+
58 Kd5 g5
59 Nd6+ Kg6
60 Kd4 Nb3+

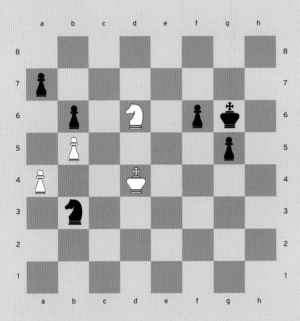

Kasparov resigned in this hopeless position. The black kingside pawns will sail down the board unopposed and there will soon be a winning promotion.

0–1

1996 brought another sensation, with Kasparov losing the first encounter of a six-game match against 'Deep Blue.' The human champion recovered well and went on to win the match 4-2, but it was highly significant that a machine could beat a World Champion in 'classical chess', as opposed to a rapidplay encounter.

Deep Blue vs. Garry Kasparov
Philadelphia, 1996

1 e4 c5
2 c3

Already an interesting moment. The machine avoids the main lines of the Sicilian Defence (2 Nf3 and 3 d4) and plays something less challenging. Kasparov equalizes easily.

2 ...d5	7 h3 Bh5
3 exd5 Qxd5	8 0-0 Nc6
4 d4 Nf6	9 Be3 cxd4
5 Nf3 Bg4	10 cxd4 Bb4
6 Be2 e6	11 a3 Ba5

Black stands well here. He will be able to complete his development by castling his king into safety and then can set about applying pressure to the isolated queen's pawn, typically with ...Bb6 and ...R(either)d8.

12 Nc3 Qd6
13 Nb5 Qe7
14 Ne5 Bxe2
15 Qxe2 0-0
16 Rac1 Rac8

This natural move is actually a slight error. Black needed to force the pace here with 16 ...a6, when 17 Nxc6 bxc6 18 Nc3 would have left the game completely equal. As played, he allows the machine to compromise the black kingside pawn structure.

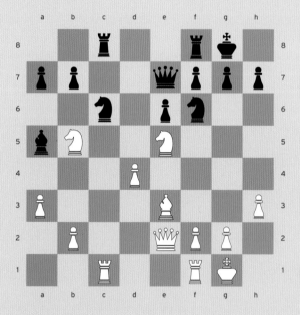

17 Bg5! Bb6
18 Bxf6 gxf6

18 ...Qxf6 keeps the pawns intact but allows a knight fork with 19 Nd7!

19 Nc4 Rfd8
20 Nxb6 axb6

White clearly has the superior pawn structure. One can imagine Kasparov, with the eyes of the world upon him, feeling very uncomfortable at this point.

21 Rfd1 f5
22 Qe3 Qf6
23 d5!

A fine move. White gets rid of his one potentially weak pawn and induces a further weakening of the black structure.

23 ...Rxd5
24 Rxd5 exd5
25 b3 Kh8
26 Qxb6 Rg8
27 Qc5 d4
28 Nd6 f4

Transposition to any endgame will lead to defeat for Kasparov because his pawn structure is shambolic. He decides to stake everything on a kingside attack. Most humans would panic in the face of a full-on Kasparov assault but the computer is quick to assess the potential level of danger and calmly proceeds to pick off weak pawns.

29 Nxb7! Ne5
30 Qd5 f3
31 g3 Nd3
32 Rc7 Re8
33 Nd6 Re1+
34 Kh2 Nxf2

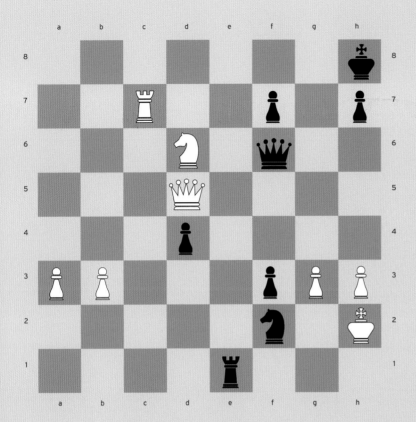

It is hard to believe that any human player would voluntarily risk this position against Kasparov. He threatens checkmate with 35 ...Rh1 and there is no way to defend that square. Yet the computer has already analyzed the position right up to a victorious conclusion.

35 Nxf7+! Kg7

Black could try 35 ...Qxf7, hoping for 36 Qxf7?? Rh1 checkmate, but 36 Qd8+! Kg7 37 Rxf7+ Kxf7 38 Qd7+ wins for White, who will pick off the f3 pawn after a few more checks (for example: 38 ...Kg6 39 Qc6+ Kg7 40 Qxf3 with an easy win, as 40 ...Rh1 is no longer checkmate).

36 Ng5+ Kh6
37 Rxh7+

Here Kasparov resigned, seeing that 37 ...Kg6 38 Qg8+ Kf5 39 Nxf3 would leave him three pawns down and faced with serious threats, such as 40

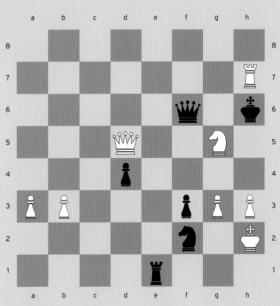

Nxe1 and 40 Rf7.
1-0

The biggest surprise of all came one year later, in 1997. Kasparov, defender of the human race, lost a match against 'Deeper Blue' by a score of $2\frac{1}{2}$- $3\frac{1}{2}$. The scores were equal after the first five games but Kasparov played very poorly in the sixth and final game.

Deeper Blue vs.
Garry Kasparov
Man vs. Machine, New York, 1997

1 e4 c6
This is already a surprise. Kasparov played the Caro-Kann Defence early in his career but the Sicilian Defence was easily his No.1 all-time favourite opening.

2 d4 d5
3 Nc3 dxe4
4 Nxe4 Nd7
5 Ng5 Ngf6
6 Bd3 e6
7 N1f3 h6??

A sensation. Kasparov plays a move which is known to be a mistake. 7 ...Bd6 followed by 8 ...h6 is much better, as the king will be able to run to f8 in some lines if White decides to sacrifice the knight.

8 Nxe6!
8 ...fxe6 9 Bg6+ Ke7 is no way for a World Champion to play, but frankly the alternative isn't much better.

8 ...Qe7
9 0-0 fxe6
10 Bg6+ Kd8
11 Bf4

Black has an extra knight, but how can he hope to complete his development and find a haven for his king?

11 ...b5
12 a4 Bb7
13 Re1 Nd5
14 Bg3 Kc8
15 axb5 cxb5
16 Qd3 Bc6
17 Bf5!

A star move, which exploits the pin on the e-pawn. Kasparov tries to relieve the pressure by exchanging his queen for two more white pieces, but it doesn't help him.

17 ...exf5
18 Rxe7 Bxe7
19 c4

The black position is a shambles and White is about to rip open more lines to get at the enemy king. Kasparov resigned right here.
1-0

Interest in Man vs. Machine contests declined sharply after Michael Adams (England's No.1) was crushed $\frac{1}{2}$-$5\frac{1}{2}$ by 'Hydra' in 2005 and Vladimir Kramnik was defeated 2-4 by 'Deep Fritz' in 2006. It is now readily accepted that computers can comfortably beat the world's strongest players. 'Deep Fritz' could already calculate 8 million positions per second back in 2006 and since then chess computer programs have not stopped improving.

The more helpful side of computers in chess comes in the form of databases and analysis engines. Serious tournament players can use enormous databases, featuring a million or more games, to prepare for future battles. They can, for example, study the games of their next opponent and work out the best way to play certain opening variations. Analysis engines help players to carefully examine their own games. These engines will instantly find tactical errors, leaving humans able to repair gaps in their knowledge with hopes of doing better next time.

KNOW YOUR OPENINGS

The theory of modern chess openings has developed rapidly over the years. Even club players - who play chess as a hobby and have no intention of becoming professionals - use computers and databases to prepare their favourite openings as deeply as possible. Some variations of popular openings have established theory lasting 20 moves and beyond. But inexperienced players need to focus on a few key principles before trying to learn openings in greater detail.

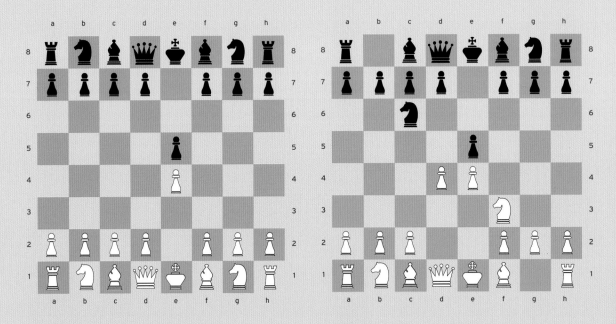

King's Pawn Openings: 1 e4...

1 ...e5 and now:

2 Nf3 Nc6 3 d4 - The Scotch Game.

A popular choice; safe and sound. After 3 ...exd4 4 Nxd4 Black has various ways to try to dislodge the centralized knight, with 4 ...Bc5 being the normal choice. White can also try 4 c3, leading to the Scotch Gambit, but it is currently out of fashion and not considered dangerous.

2 Nf3 Nc6 3 Bb5: The Spanish Game (or Ruy Lopez).

The most popular of all king's pawn openings and the one with the most chance of providing White with an advantage against strong players. We will look more closely at the Spanish Game on pages 157–61.

2 Nf3 Nc6 3 Bc4 Be7: The Hungarian Defence.

Solid but passive for Black. His king's bishop is clearly more actively placed on c5 than e7.

2 Nf3 Nc6 3 Bc4 Bc5: The Italian Game (or Giuoco Piano).

Very safe but regarded as less challenging than the Spanish and Scotch openings. White can play 4 c3 and follow up with 5 d4 (to occupy the centre) or 5 d3 (to calmly develop before undertaking any further action in the centre). He can also try 4 b4 – the Evans Gambit. The idea is to deflect Black from the centre (4 ...Bxb4) and then try to occupy it with c3 and d4. It was popular in the days of Steinitz but very rarely seen these days.

2 Nf3 Nc6 3 Bc4 Nf6: The Two Knights Defence.

Black invites sharp play after 4 Ng5 d5 5 exd5 Na5 or even 4 Ng5 Bc5!? – the risky Traxler Counter-Attack, Both players need to know their theory to avoid a disaster. White can head back to the Italian Game with 5 d3 if he is unsure how to handle the complications.

2 Nf3 Nc6 3 Nc3 Nf6: The Four Knights Game.

Very solid for both sides. Considered dull and drawish as Black can copy White's moves for some time and usually gain rapid equality.

2 Nf3 Nf6: The Petroff Defence (or Russian Defence).

A very popular defence for Black. It was considered drawish for many years, until White found some interesting ways to sharpen the play, usually by castling on the queenside and using his kingside pawns to launch an attack on the black king.

2 Nf3 d6: Philidor's Defence.

Considered somewhat passive for Black, because his king's bishop is blocked in. There are some exciting lines where Black plays 3 ...f5, but these are considered very risky for him.

2 f4: The King's Gambit.

The most popular opening in the days of Greco and it remained a respectable choice well into the 1800s. It is no longer considered dangerous for Black, but he has to know his lines to avoid coming under a fearsome attack.

2 d4 exd4 3 c3: The Danish Gambit.

White offers to sacrifice two pawns for the initiative. After 3 ...dxc3 4 Bc4 cxb2 5 Bxb2 White can develop a strong attack, if Black is not careful. Giving some of the material back with 5...d5!, to ensure Black will catch up with development, takes much of the sting out of White's intentions. The Danish Gambit is very rarely played these days.

2 d4 exd4 3 Qxd4: The Centre Game.

Never popular. White's queen has come out too soon and Black will be able to exploit it as a target as he develops his pieces, starting with 3 ...Nc6.

1 e4 e5 2 Bc4: The Bishop's Opening.

A sound alternative to the Spanish Game, although it doesn't give White as much chance of gaining the initiative. Black should be able to equalize the game without too much difficulty.

1 e4 e5 2 Nc3: The Vienna Game.

Play often transposes to the Bishop's Opening after an early Bc4. Again, Black should be able to equalize with sensible developing moves.

1 e4 e5 2 Nc3 Nf6 3 f4: The Vienna Gambit.

White combines ideas from the Vienna Game with those of the King's Gambit. One difference is that accepting the gambit with 3 ...exf4 (perfectly good in the King's Gambit) is inadvisable here due to 4 e5! and the black knight has to return to g8. Black should play the classic central counter 3 ...d5! with an equal game.

1 ...c5: The Sicilian Defence.

Black's most popular alternative to 1 ...e5. This will be covered in more detail later on.

1 ...e6: The French Defence.

Very solid. We will cover this defence in more detail later in the book.

1 ...c6: The Caro-Kann Defence.

Another very reliable opening, similar in style to the French Defence. Black will play 2 ...d5 to put the white centre under immediate pressure.

1 e4 d5: The Scandinavian Defence (sometimes called the Centre Counter).

This has become more popular over the last decade or so, despite the very early development of the black queen after 2 exd5 Qxd5 (2 ...Nf6 is also possible, intending to recapture on d5 with the knight). It requires careful handling.

1 e4 Nc6: The Nimzowitsch Defence.

An unpopular opening. After 2 d4 Black has two choices: 2 ...d5 and 2 ...e5. Both are difficult to handle and White should be able to retain an edge.

1 ...Nf6: Alekhine's Defence.

At first glance, this seems a ridiculous move. The idea is to let White chase the knight around with his pawns. Black will then try to destroy White's pawn centre. This opening is risky and difficult to handle, although it has been used occasionally at World Championship level.

1 ...g6: The Modern Defence.

It is possible to play 1 ...g6 against any of White's first moves. Once considered a 'joke opening' - because it allows White unrestricted freedom in the centre - it is now frequently seen and considered perfectly respectable. Black obviously intends 2 ...Bg7, after which he will set about trying to undermine whatever set up in the centre White chooses to adopt.

1 e4 d6 2 d4 Nf6 followed by 3 ...g6: The Pirc Defence.

The Pirc and Modern Defences have very similar ideas and often transpose into each other.

1 e4 a6: The St. George Defence.

The idea is similar to the Modern Defence: to allow White to occupy the centre and then to undermine it. The English International Master, Mike Basman, is the world's leading pioneer of the St. George. (He also runs the UK Junior Chess Challenge – the biggest chess tournament in the world).

The St. George Defence received a boost when England's first Grandmaster, Tony Miles, used it to beat Anatoly Karpov (the reigning World Champion at the time) in 1980. However, it has yet to enjoy widespread recognition and is very rarely seen in tournament chess.

Queen's Pawn Openings: 1 d4...

1 ...d5 and now...

2 c4: The Queen's Gambit.

2 c4 e6:The Queen's Gambit Declined.

A very popular opening. We will cover it in further detail later in the book. We will deal with the Catalan Opening there too (**1 d4 d5 2 c4 e6 3 g3**).

2 c4 e6 3 Nc3 (or 3 Nf3) c5: The Tarrasch Defence.

Black can obtain dynamic play with this early advance, but he has to accept an isolated queen's pawn after 4 cxd5 exd5 and an eventual trade of his c-pawn for White's d-pawn. Some players do not like to have isolated pawns (because they could become weak later in the game), consequently, the Tarrasch Defence has always struggled to enjoy the popularity of the more solid main lines of the Queen's Gambit. However, it is a good choice for club players who welcome active piece play as Black.

2 c4 dxc4: The Queen's Gambit Accepted.

Never as popular as the Queen's Gambit Declined but perfectly acceptable nonetheless. It allows White to construct an ideal centre (with either 3 e4 – followed by Bxc4 – or with 3 Nf3, 4 e3 and a

later e3-e4). Black needs to handle this opening carefully to succeed.

2 c4 c6: The Slav Defence.

Very solid and popular. Black declines the Queen's Gambit but plays to keep his queen's bishop active. There are some sharper lines if Black plays an early ...e6 (the Semi-Slav) instead of developing his bishop.

2 c4 e5: The Albin Counter-Gambit.

Black not only declines the Queen's Gambit; he offers a gambit of his own in return. It is risky and has never been popular but it can be an effective surprise weapon for special occasions.

1 d4 Nf6 and now...

2 c4 e6 3 Nc3 Bb4: The Nimzo-Indian Defence.

Possibly the best of all the Indian defences (so called because Black's pawns move only one square during the first few moves, as if he is playing by the old Indian rules). We will look at the Nimzo-Indian again later in the book.

2 c4 e6 3 Nf3 b6: The Queen's Indian Defence.

This is the natural brother to the Nimzo-Indian. Note the difference in White's knight moves; the Nimzo-Indian is used against 3 Nc3 and the Queen's Indian against 3 Nf3. It is very solid indeed and one of the most reliable of all Black's opening choices.

2 c4 e6 3 Nf3 Bb4+: The Bogo-Indian Defence.

A sound alternative to the Queen's Indian Defence. A related opening is the Keres System (1 d4 e6 2 c4 Bb4+) into which the game can easily transpose.

2 c4 e6 3 Nc3 (or 3 Nf3) c5: The Modern Benoni Defence.

Very sharp. Black will have to try to break down a big white centre, usually by tactical means. It is aggressive and difficult to handle.

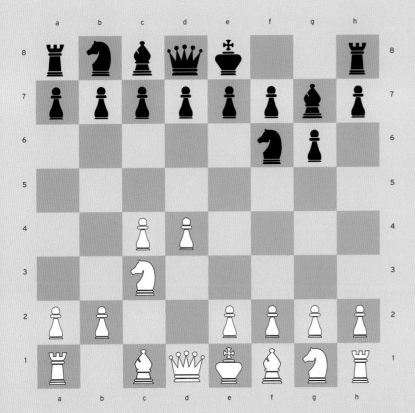

2 c4 g6 3 Nc3 Bg7: The King's Indian Defence.

Similar to the Pirc and Modern Defences. Black will once again have to break down a big pawn centre. It is safer and more popular than the Benoni, but requires careful handling and a good memory, because the theoretical lines can be extensive.

2 c4 g6 3 Nc3 d5: The Grunfeld Defence.

This defence is very much in fashion with top Grandmasters. Once again Black allows White to build a centre and then will seek to destroy it. One main line starts with 4 cxd5 Nxd5 5 e4 Nxc36 bxc3 and Black will attack the centre with ...c5, ...Bg7, ...Nc6 and ...Qa5. As with the King's Indian, there are long lines of theory which may prove difficult for inexperienced players to understand.

2 c4 c5 3 d5 b5: The Benko Gambit.

Black sacrifices a pawn to gain activity and open lines for his major pieces. Play typically continues: 4 cxb5 a6 5 bxa6 Bxa6 and the black rooks will eventually sit side by side on a8 and b8, from where they will place the white queenside pawns under tremendous pressure (usually augmented by the king's bishop, posted on g7). The Benko Gambit is a good weapon for club players but has never been particularly popular with top Grandmasters.

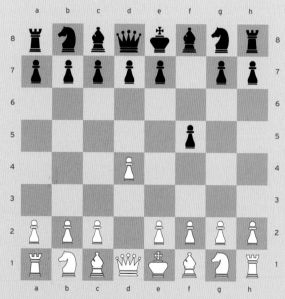

1 d4 f5: The Dutch Defence.

An ambitious defence. Black seizes space in the centre but weakens his king's position. Some people love it, others loathe it. It's difficult to handle, especially for inexperienced players, although a Dutch Defence specialist will achieve success with it against ill-prepared 1 d4 players.

1 d4 followed by 2 Nf3 and 3 Bf4: The London System.

White aims for sensible development before attempting to gain an advantage. The moves e3, Bd3, c3, Nbd2 and 0-0 usually follow.

1 d4 followed by 2 Nf3 and 3 e3: The Colle System.

A system related to the London and with similar intentions, but here the queen's bishop often goes to b2.

1 d4 followed by 2 Nf3 and 3 Bg5: The Torre Attack.

Another universal system for White (it can also be played against 2 ...g6). The Torre, Colle and London are considered relatively harmless at Grandmaster level but as they can be learnt quickly and are easy to understand, they represent safe and sound choices for club players and novices.

1 d4 Nf6 2 Bg5: The Trompowsky Attack.

Quite popular in English chess circles for the last 20 years, without ever becoming established as a major opening, the Trompowsky leads to original play and can be an effective surprise weapon.

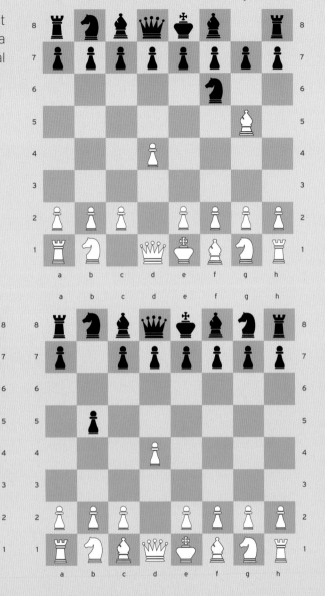

1 d4 followed by 2 e3 and an early f4: The Stonewall Attack.

This is, effectively the Dutch Defence (Stonewall Variation) as played by White, who can build up a powerful kingside attack against unwary opponents. Nevertheless, it is very rarely seen at Grandmaster level.

1 d4 b5: The Polish Defence.

An eccentric opening and a very unpopular choice. Black impedes the white c-pawn but cedes central control. It can transpose into the St. George Defence after 2 e4 b5.

Other Openings

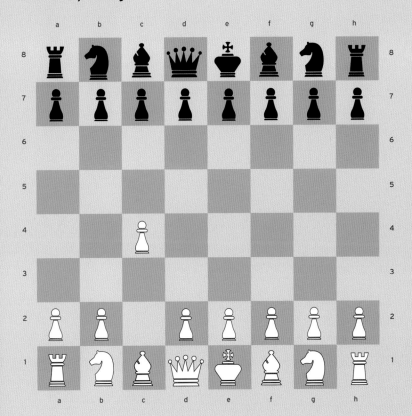

1 c4 The English Opening.

Nearly all of the World Champions have used the English Opening at some point in their careers. It is probably the third most common opening move (after 1 e4 and 1 d4). White usually continues with Nc3, Nf3, g3, Bg2 and 0-0 with an extremely solid position.

1 Nf3: The Reti Opening.

This can easily transpose into a number of other openings (for example, an early c2-c4 by White can lead back into the English Opening). The traditional Reti plan involves g3, Bg2, 0-0 before committing any central pawns.

1 b3: The Nimzo-Larsen Attack.

Sometimes White plays 1 Nf3 first and then 2 b3. Never universally popular, the Nimzo-Larsen Attack has some tricky ideas but Black should be fine whether he replies with 1 ...d5 or 1 ...e5.

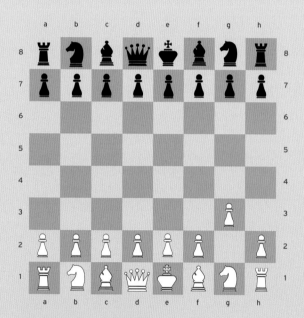

1 g3: The Benko Opening.

This usually transposes to the Reti or English Opening.

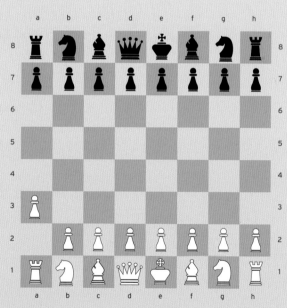

1 a3: Anderssen's Opening.

An eccentric opening. The idea is to continue, after 1 ...e5, with 2 e4, when after 2 ...Nf6 3 Nc3 Black can't play 3 ...Bb4 with a reversed Spanish Opening. This relic from the 1800s is now one of the rarest of all openings.

1 b4: The Orangutan Opening (sometimes called the Sokolsky Opening).

Another unusual opening. White aims to play Bb2 as quickly as possible but the advanced b-pawn can prove to be more of a liability than a strength, because when it is attacked White will have to waste a move, either advancing the pawn or protecting it. 1 b4 is very rarely seen and not considered dangerous.

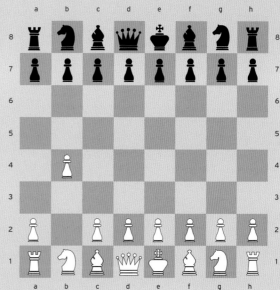

1 g4: Grob's Opening.

1 g4 is another opening tested repeatedly by International Master Mike Basman. He even likes to employ it with Black (1 e4 g5). It has never been popular and it takes a certain type of player to play it successfully. White can also play 1 h3 as a way to play a Grob by a slightly different order of moves. Two more rare moves are 1 c3 and 1 e3, both of which will usually transpose into other openings.

As chess players become more experienced, they will find some openings suit their personal styles much more than others. I would like to highlight six popular openings that have all stood the test of time and which will serve players faithfully over a long period of time.

These openings, accompanied by their respective heroes, are:

For White:
The Spanish Game/Ruy Lopez (Bobby Fischer)
The Queen's Gambit (Alexander Alekhine)
The Catalan (Vladimir Kramnik)

For Black:
The French Defence (Viktor Korchnoi)
The Sicilian Defence (Garry Kasparov)
The Nimzo-Indian Defence (Anatoly Karpov)

The French Defence

The French Defence is one of the most solid and reliable openings at Black's disposal. After White's most popular first move **1 e4** Black replies with **1 e6**.

The basic idea is to allow White to construct a centre with **2 d4** and then challenge it immediately by **2 ...d5**.

White's e-pawn is under attack and he must make an early decision, which will determine the subsequent course of the game.

He can play...

a) 3 exd5 The Exchange Variation, which is generally thought to be harmless. Black simply replies with **3 ...exd5** and obtains an equal position (a notable achievement after just three moves).

b) 3 e5

The Advance Variation. White intends to keep his centre in one piece and hopes that the pawn on e5 will restrict Black's development. Black's plan is to challenge the centre as soon as possible with the idea of dismantling it completely. The first step along this path will be 3 ...c5.

c) 3 Nc3

Defending the e-pawn, whilst simultaneously developing a piece. Black has several ways to respond. **3 ...dxe4** (Rubinstein Variation) punches a hole in White's centre but is considered somewhat passive. Both **3 ...Nf6** (Classical Variation) and **3 ...Bb4** (Winawer Variation) renew the central pressure and activate a piece at the same time.

d) 3 Nd2

The Tarrasch Variation. White defends the e-pawn and develops a piece – whilst preventing the challenging Winawer Variation. Black's two most common moves here are **3 ...Nf6 and 3 ...c5**, once again aiming at White's central pawns.

Viktor Korchnoi –
Hero of the French Defence

Viktor Korchnoi is one of the greatest heroes of the French Defence. He never quite made it to be World Champion but was a serious title contender on numerous occasions. The closest he came was a 5-6 defeat to Anatoly Karpov in 1978.

Korchnoi, who continued playing chess at a high level into his 80s, produced many famous victories in the French Defence. In the following game he achieves the aim of destroying the white centre by means of Black's two standard pawn breaks (8 ...c5 and 12 ...f6). Black's own central pawns are then able to advance and create chaos in the enemy camp.

Paul Van der Sterren vs. Viktor Korchnoi
Wijk aan Zee, 1984

1 e4 e6
2 d4 d5
3 Nc3 Nf6
4 Bg5 Be7

At this point, Black can also try 4 ...dxe4 (Burn Variation - similar to the Rubinstein Variation, 3 ...dxe4), but the text is more combative.

The initial moves are all about the battle for the centre. Black is forcing White to decide what to do about his e-pawn. If he plays 5 exd5 then Black will have an equal game after 5 ...exd5. 5 Bxf6 would relieve some of the pressure but most players are reluctant to exchange a bishop for a knight so early in the game – as having 'the two bishops' against a bishop and a knight is considered to be an advantage. So White advances the pawn, after which both sides will focus on the central pawns e5 and d4. White will try hard to keep them in place, while Black must try to undermine them.

5 e5 Nfd7
6 Bxe7 Qxe7
7 f4 0-0
8 Nf3 c5

9 dxc5 Qxc5
10 Qd2 Nb6
11 Nb5 Nc6
12 c3 f6

Black's second major pawn break. If White doesn't capture on f6 then Black will play 13 ...fxe5, leaving White with a very weak and isolated pawn on e5, which will come under enormous pressure.

13 exf6 Rxf6
Who has the big pawn centre now?
14 Bd3 Nc4
15 Bxc4 Qxc4
16 Nbd4 Bd7
17 b3 Qa6
18 0-0-0 Nxd4
19 Nxd4 Raf8
20 g3

The move 8 ...c5 shows one of Black's main ideas in the battle for the centre. Note how White cannot defend the d4 pawn with another pawn, as the knight on c3 prevents him from playing c2-c3. Note also that Black is ready to play 9 ...Nc6 if White doesn't capture the pawn. Black should delay the development of the queen's knight until his c-pawn has advanced to c5, otherwise this pawn will be impeded and unable to attack the centre.

With all of Black's pieces developed, Korchnoi seizes the opportunity to open up the game. White's rook on h1 is still undeveloped and his king looks a little draughty (it is inadvisable to move pawns in front of a castled king) so any tactics are likely to favour Black.

20 ...e5

A very powerful move. If White accepts the sacrifice with 21 fxe5 then he loses quickly after 21...Rf2. The problem then is that if he moves his queen away from the attack (for example, 22 Qd3) then Black forces a checkmate in two moves. Can you see how?

Analysis diagram

21 Ne2 d4
22 cxd4 Bg4

Using a pin to increase the pressure.

23 Rde1 Rc6+
24 Kb2 Rfc8

The black rooks have skipped across from the f-file to the c-file. It is easy to see that Black has a big advantage here.

25 Nc1 Bf5

With the threat of 26 ...Rc2+.

26 Qb4 Rb6

26 ...Rc2+ is even stronger but Black is winning either way.

27 Qe7 Qa5

Threatening a deadly check by the queen on c3. White's next move is an attempt to create some space for his king, but there is to be no escape.

28 a4 Qxa4

The queen cannot be captured because the rook on b6 pins the pawn on b3. White has no satisfactory way of preventing 29 ...Rc2+ so he resigned. **0-1**

Laurent Fressinet vs. Viktor Korchnoi

Cannes, 1996

1 e4 e6
2 d4 d5
3 e5 c5

The battle lines are already drawn. White will try to keep the centre intact, which will ensure he has more space to manoeuvre and leave the opponent cramped. Meanwhile Black will try to dismantle the white pawn structure, reckoning it to be an easy target.

4 c3 Nc6
5 Nf3 Qb6
6 a3 Nh6

A provocative idea, which is very much in Korchnoi's style. Bringing a knight to the side of the board is usually considered inferior ("a knight on the rim is dim") but the idea is to bring it quickly to f5, in order to apply more pressure on the white centre. Black is prepared to allow the splintering of his kingside pawn structure if White should decide to exchange bishop for knight.

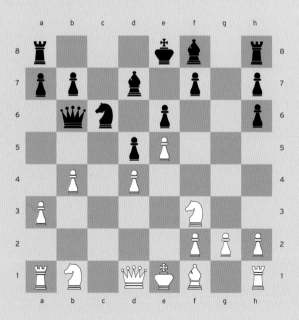

position after 9 ...Bd7

7 b4 cxd4
8 Bxh6 gxh6
9 cxd4 Bd7

Both players must have been happy at this point. White's proud centre remains intact while Black's kingside has been severely compromised. However, in return, Korchnoi has the bishop pair and plenty of pieces ready to attack the centre. It's worth spending some time looking at ways in which White can try to attack the kingside pawns. Without a dark-squared bishop, the h6 pawn is very difficult to attack and if White lines up on the h7 pawn - with Bd3 and Qc2 - then his d4 pawn will be left with insufficient defence. So it is remarkably difficult to mount a successful assault on the kingside and so Black's king is relatively safe there.

There is clearly sufficient imbalance in the position for both sides to play for a win. The next few moves see the two players continue to develop their pieces to the most obvious squares.

10 Be2 Rc8
11 0-0 Bg7
12 Qd2 0-0
13 Nc3

How should Korchnoi continue? 13 ...f6 looks logical. After 14 exf6 Rxf6 (not 14 ...Bxf6? Because of 15 Qxh6) White might continue with 15 Na4, forcing the queen to move and then continuing

16 Nc5 with a slight advantage due to his extra space. Korchnoi finds something far more challenging.

13 ...Nxd4!

A temporary sacrifice which enables Korchnoi to smash up the white centre.

14 Nxd4 Bxe5
15 Rad1 Bxd4

White has tactical problems. The knight on d4 is under attack, but if it moves (to f3, for example) then Black will simply capture the knight on c3 and remain two pawns up (an easy win for a Grandmaster). If White tries 16 Ndb5 to protect the other knight, then 16 ...a6 proves embarrassing as there is no sensible retreat. 16 Ncb5 Bxb5 17 Nxb5 a6 is another try which ends up very favourable for Black. So White finds a clever way to limit his losses to a single pawn, by means of a desperado sacrifice.

16 Nxd5 Bxf2+

Black uses a desperado too.

17 Rxf2 exd5
18 Qxd5 Ba4

The smoke has cleared and Black is a pawn up. His king is looking a little draughty now that he has lost his dark-squared bishop, so he rushes to plug some of the gaps with his other bishop.

19 Rdf1 Bc2
20 Kh1 Bg6
21 h4 Rc1

Ensuring a swap of one pair of rooks. Exchanging pieces suits Black better than White, because he is ahead in material and the reduction of forces makes it harder for White to attack.

22 Qf3 Rxf1+
23 Rxf1 Re8
24 h5 Re4!

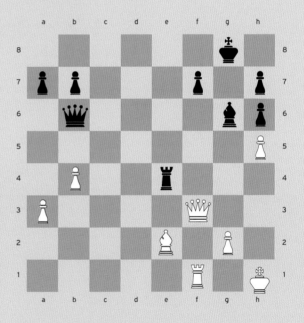

If Black had moved the bishop then White would have captured on f7 with checkmate to follow after just two more moves. Korchnoi once again demonstrates his counterattacking skill. If now 25 hxg6?? then 25 ...Rh4+ forces White to interpose with his queen, leading to a lost position.

25 g3 Re3!
26 Qg4

If 26 Qf2 – retaining the pressure on f7 – Black's bishop joins the attack with 26 ...Be4+ followed by 27 ...Bd5, defending f7. Black will then be free to attack the weakened white king. After 26 Qg4 it looks as if the pinned black bishop will be lost, but Korchnoi has other ideas.

26 ...Qc6+

White should now try 27 Kg1 and look for ways to defend after 27 ...Qc3 (threatening 28 ...Rxg3+). After the inferior 27 Kh2, Black has the strong resource 27 ...Qe4! However, the move he plays in the game is the weakest of all. It's so easy to make a mistake when under pressure.

27 Bf3??

27 ...Rxf3!
28 Rxf3

28 Qxf3?? is even worse, as it allows the pin with 28 ...Be4!

28 ...f5!

This is probably what White missed. The queen has to continue protecting the rook, but to do so she has to unpin the black bishop...

29 Qf4 Bxh5

...which once again is free to attack the pinned rook. White can defend the rook again with 30 Kg2 but this leads to a hopeless position after 30 ...Qxf3+ 31 Qxf3 Bxf3+ 32 Kxf3 when the extra black pawns will win the game. So White resigned.
0-1

Stefano Tatai vs. Viktor Korchnoi
Beersheba, 1978

1 e4 e6
2 d4 d5
3 exd5 exd5

If you play the French Defence you will definitely encounter the Exchange Variation from time to time. Usually it is adopted by a player who is happy to draw the game. However, there are still plenty of ways to complicate matters.

4 Bd3 c5

Korchnoi quickly unbalances the position. This will provide him with more opportunities to outplay his opponent. Black is happy to exchange his c-pawn for the white d-pawn, even though he will be left with an isolated queen's pawn ('IQP'). In an endgame this could turn out to be a weakness because it cannot be defended by other pawns, but in the middlegame it will grant Black extra space in the centre and free play for his pieces.

position after 12 Nbd2

5 Nf3 Nc6
6 Qe2+ Be7
7 dxc5 Nf6
8 h3 0-0
9 0-0 Bxc5
10 c3 Re8
11 Qc2 Qd6
12 Nbd2

All normal-looking play so far, but Korchnoi's next move is very surprising.

12 ...Qg3!!

Suddenly White is in big trouble. By exploiting the pin on the f2 pawn (by the bishop on c5) Black's queen is able to penetrate deep into White's position. The immediate threat is 13 ...Bxh3, exploiting another pin (by the queen on the g-pawn). White is able to stop that threat but only at the cost of a further weakening of his position.

13 Bf5 Re2!

Applying even more pressure to the pinned f2-pawn. The threat is simply 14 ...Rxf2.

14 Nd4

Breaking the pin on the f2-pawn, which places the black queen under attack and threatens the rook on e2. It sounds good, but Black is still in complete control.

14 ...Nxd4!

A very strong reply. Neither 15 cxd4 Bxd4 - re-establishing the deadly pin - nor 15 fxg3 Nxc2+ can stop the black attack from crashing through, so White decided to resign.

0-1

Sergey Kudrin vs. Viktor Korchnoi
Beersheba, 1984

1 e4 e6
2 d4 d5
3 Nd2

The Tarrasch Variation is very popular. White aims to keep control of the centre and establish a slight but enduring advantage.

3 ...Nf6

Korchnoi played 3 ...c5 consistently against Anatoly Karpov in two famous matches, in 1974 and 1978, drawing every time. In this game he chooses the other main line.

4 e5 Nfd7
5 c3 c5
6 Bd3 Nc6
7 Ne2 cxd4
8 cxd4 f6

Once again we see the recurring theme of destroying the centre with the ...c5 and ...f6 breaks.

9 exf6 Nxf6
10 Nf3 Bd6
11 0-0 Qc7
12 Nc3 a6

Beginners often waste time with irrelevant pawn moves, especially those of the a- and h-pawns. When Grandmasters play such moves it is invariably with good reason. Here, it was important to stop 13 Nb5! which would have enabled White to trade his knight for Black's good dark-squared bishop. White tries to find another way to swap off the bishop, but again he is thwarted.

13 Bg5 0-0
14 Bh4 Nh5!

White was hoping to play 15 Bg3, followed by exchanging the dark-squared bishops. However, Korchnoi wants to keep his bishop on the board and so prepares to meet 15 Bg3 with 15 ...Nxg3.

15 Re1 g6
An interesting plan. Korchnoi is going to apply more pressure on the d4-pawn with his queen.

16 Rc1 Qg7
17 Bb1 Bd7
18 Bg3 Nxg3
19 hxg3

Korchnoi now finds another way to increase the pressure.

19 ...g5!
The plan is to double rooks on the f-file and then chase away the defending knight with ...g4, leading to the collapse of f2.

20 Qd3 Rf7
21 Rcd1 Raf8
22 Rd2 Kh8
23 Nd1 Bc7
24 Qe3
Trying to force Black to make a decision with the g-pawn. Should he push it to g4 (which White wouldn't mind, as the f2 pawn is sufficiently defended even when the knight moves) or

defend it with 24 ...h6, which may weaken the king's defence? Neither! Korchnoi is quick to spot a tactical solution.

24 ...Rxf3!!
25 gxf3 Bf4
Now if 26 Qd3 (or 26 Qc3, which comes to the same thing) 26 ...Bxd2 27 Qxd2 Nxd4 and White's centre has completely collapsed. And even worse news: he cannot stop a devastating knight fork (28 ...Nxf3) on the next move, so he resigned.
0-1

The Sicilian Defence

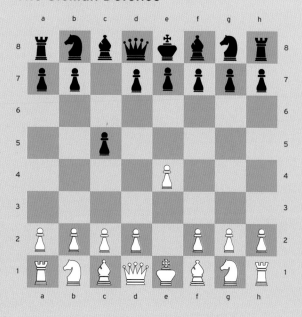

1 e4 c5

The Sicilian Defence is extremely popular at all levels of play. The basic ideas are easy to understand and inexperienced players can try it out. However, when playing it against more experienced opponents, greater theoretical knowledge is needed than when playing the French Defence. White can develop dangerous attacks early in the game and Black has to know his stuff to be able to stay in the game. But if Black knows the theory behind the sharp lines then he has every chance of repulsing any attacks and taking over the initiative in the late middlegame or even the endgame.

White's most challenging lines start after the following moves.

2 Nf3 d6 3 d4 cxd4 4 Nxd4 Nf6 5 Nc3

Black had several choices on his second move, with 2 ...Nc6, 2 ...e6, 2 ...a6, 2 ...Nf6 and 2 ...g6 all leading to recognized lines. However, 2 ...d6 is an especially popular choice as it can lead to the Dragon (5 ...g6) and Najdorf (5 ... a6) variations, both of which lead to sharp and challenging play.

As White has more space in the centre, he will find it easy to develop his pieces to good squares. He will then launch an attack in the early middlegame. Black has more central pawns, which will help him control key squares, and

he enjoys the half-open c-file, which he will use for his rooks and queen to exert considerable pressure on the white queenside. It is precisely the unbalanced nature of the position that makes it an ideal choice for a fighting player.

White has ways of avoiding the main lines and a Sicilian player needs to know some of the theory about each one in order to play the defence with confidence. Our illustrative games will focus on encounters featuring the main lines, but players wanting to add 1 e4 c5 to their repertoire will need to research the following lines.

1 e4 c5 2 c3 (Alapin Variation)
White's idea is to avoid ending up with fewer central pawns than Black. He plans 3 d4 and if Black replies with 3 cxd4 then White will play 4 cxd4, with a powerful centre. Black players usually try to avoid White's intention. 2 ...Nf6 and 2 ...d5 are common moves, both challenging the e4 pawn.

1 e4 c5 2 Nf3 d6 3 Bb5+ (Moscow Variation)

1 e4 c5 2 Nf3 Nc6 3 Bb5 (Rossolimo Variation)

The Moscow and Rossolimo Variations are closely related. White intends to avoid the long main lines of the Sicilian and tries to obtain a slight but steady initiative. The Rossolimo Variation has become more popular in recent years, as there are some potent plans involving an early Bxc6, compromising Black's pawn structure.

1 e4 c5 2 Nc3 with either **3 g3** (Closed Sicilian) or **3 f4** (Grand Prix Attack) to follow, are other systems. White will push his kingside pawns with the intention of launching a strong attack against the opponent's king.

Garry Kasparov – Hero of the Sicilian Defence

Garry Kasparov is undoubtedly one of the greatest of all chess players. He rose rapidly through the ranks and became the youngest ever World Champion in 1985, when he defeated Anatoly Karpov in a tough title match. He remained champion until he lost his crown to Vladimir Kramnik in 2000.

Throughout his chess career, Kasparov remained faithful to his favourite Sicilian Defence. Indeed, Karpov, one of the most effective Sicilian slayers, ultimately failed to crack Kasparov's defence and eventually stopped playing 1 e4 altogether.

Kasparov went on to use the Sicilian Defence to defend his title in exciting matches against Nigel Short (1993) and Viswanathan Anand (1995), and against all of the world's top players in a wide range of very strong tournaments. Even though the Sicilian Defence invariably leads to sharp play, Kasparov very rarely lost after 1 e4 c5.

This game - against another World Champion - is a typical example of Kasparov's Sicilian Defence in action. Topalov is a top class player who is particularly strong when on the attack. Yet in this game he never seems able to create any serious threats and Black's consistent play makes everything look easy.

Veselin Topalov vs. Garry Kasparov
Euwe Memorial, Amsterdam, 1995

1 e4 c5	6 Be3 Nf6
2 Nf3 Nc6	7 f3 Be7
3 d4 cxd4	8 g4 0-0
4 Nxd4 e6	9 Qd2 a6
5 Nc3 d6	

This was Kasparov's favourite kind of Sicilian position. Black's pawns on a6, d6 and e6 act like the spines of a hedgehog. White clearly has more space but if he advances too soon or without due care and attention he will find the spines deadly.

10 0-0-0 Nxd4
11 Bxd4 b5

When the players castle on opposite sides of the board the standard plan is to launch direct attacks against each other's kings. Such attacks usually feature pawns, marching forward to create weaknesses and disruption in the enemy camp. Both players play very directly over the next few moves.

12 Kb1 Bb7
13 h4 Rc8
14 g5 Nd7
15 Rg1 b4

It is important for Black to be able to shift the white knight from c3 as this will partially clear the c-file for his rook. Much of Black's play in the Sicilian Defence comes precisely on this file.

16 Ne2 Ne5
17 Rg3 Nc4

White can win a pawn here with 18 Qxb4 but generally speaking it is a bad idea to open up lines leading towards one's own king. Black would very quickly place one rook on the b-file and the other on the c-file, with an attack so strong that it is clearly worth more than a pawn.

18 Qc1 e5
19 Bf2 a5
20 Bg2 Ba6
21 Re1 a4
22 Bh3 Rc6
23 Qd1

Black has made good progress but White's attack

on the kingside has stalled. Topalov couldn't seem to find the correct balance between pursuing his own attack and defending against Kasparov's. The latter now uses a temporary pawn sacrifice to give his pieces more energy for the push towards victory.

23 ...d5!
The last of Black's hedgehog spines moves forward.

24 exd5 Rd6!
Ensuring he will regain the pawn. White's queen will now find things very uncomfortable as she ends up on the same line as the black rook.

25 f4 Rxd5
26 Rd3
26 ...Na3+!
Unleashing a discovered attack on the rook (from the bishop on a6) and creating a huge weakness in the white position.

27 bxa3 Bxd3
28 cxd3 Rxd3
White's queen and bishop are forked and he faces great material losses. Topalov resigned.
0-1

In the next game, Kasparov produced a major surprise in a very important game. He switched from his favourite hedgehog set-up to the Sicilian Dragon. He'd never played it before and it took Anand by surprise.

Viswanathan Anand vs. Garry Kasparov
PCA World Championship, New York, 1995

1 e4 c5
2 Nf3 d6
3 d4 cxd4
4 Nxd4 Nf6
5 Nc3 g6

The famous Dragon variation. Black's bishop intends to breathe fire down the long diagonal. This will help him attack not only the centre but also White's king if it should castle on the queenside. Back in 1995, the Dragon was considered risky but this game helped to make it popular once more.

6 Be3 Bg7
7 Qd2 Nc6
8 f3 0-0
9 Bc4 Bd7
10 h4

Anand is playing the tried and trusted Yugoslav Attack. The plan is simply to checkmate Black as soon as possible, by playing a timely Bh6, exchanging the Dragon bishop (Bxg7), opening the h-file with h4-h5 (as a pawn sacrifice) and then moving in for the kill with Qh6 (backed up by the rook on h1). Many Dragon players have been crushed by this standard plan.

10 ...h5

Normally it is a bad idea to meet a pawn storm with your own pawns but this highly sophisticated idea – known as the Soltis Variation – is far more robust than it looks. White's h-pawn has been stopped in its tracks and if he now plays 11 g4 Black will just ignore it. A further push with g4-g5 will leave the kingside pawns locked and White will not have any open files on which to launch his attack. Finally, if play continues with 11 g4 and 12 gxh5 then Black will simply recapture with the knight (12 ...Nxh5), keeping the important h-file closed for a little longer and buying important time to pursue his own attack.

11 Bb3 Rc8

Black is limbering up for 12 ...Ne5 and 13 ...Nc4, annoying the bishops. Anand's intended solution is a mistake, as it strengthens the black centre.

12 Nxc6? bxc6
13 Bh6 c5
14 Bc4 Qb6
15 Bxg7 Kxg7

White has achieved something; he has swapped off the famous Dragon bishop. However, he has no immediate hope of getting his queen on to the h6 square and it is not so easy for him to find a safe place for his own king. This turns out to be a fatal weakness.

16 b3 Be6
17 Nd5 Bxd5
18 exd5

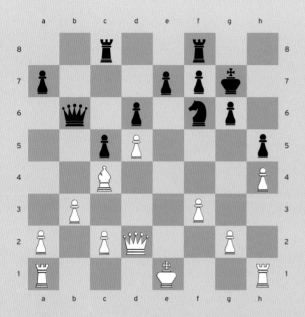

8 ...e5!

A typical thrust by Kasparov, similar to his 23 d5! against Topalov. Now White should really decide on which side he would like to castle, but instead he makes a mistake by capturing the pawn. Perhaps he was worried about ending up with a bad bishop as it is stuck on the white squares and lacking in scope because nearly all of his pawns are also on white squares. But, in any event, allowing Black to open up the game is definitely a mistake.

19 dxe6? d5!
20 Be2

20 Bxd5? runs into a deadly pin after 20 ...Rfd8.

20 ...c4
21 c3 Rce8
22 bxc4 Rxe6
23 Kf1 Rfe8
24 Bd3 dxc4
25 Bxc4

25 ...Ne4!

There is a major threat of a knight fork on g3 and White's queen is under attack too. If White tries the obvious 26 fxe4 then he will not survive for long after 26 ...Rf6+, after which the white king is helpless. Anand now resigned.

0-1

The next game was played in Kasparov's last serious tournament. To the surprise of the chess world, he announced his retirement from competitive play at the end of the event. He then entered Russian politics but retained his interest in chess through extensive literary and promotional work on the game.

Playing against England's No.1 player is never an easy task, but Kasparov's trusty Sicilian Defence once again proves to be a formidable weapon.

**Michael
Adams
vs. Garry
Kasparov**
*Linares,
2005*

1 e4 c5
2 Nf3 d6
3 d4 cxd4
4 Nxd4 Nf6
5 Nc3 a6

Kasparov often used the Najdorf Variation as a route to his favourite hedgehog system.

6 Be3 e6	12 axb4 Nxb4
7 Be2 Qc7	13 g4 Be7
8 Qd2 b5	14 g5 Nd7
9 a3 Bb7	15 h4 Nc5
10 f3 Nc6	16 Kb1 Rb8
11 0-0-0 b4	17 h5 0-0

An exciting position. Black's solid hedgehog spines have allowed him to delay castling for some time. Both attacks look strong. Who would you rather be here? A difficult choice!

18 g6! Bf6
It would have been foolish to open up the h-file with 18 ...hxg6 but the attempt to keep the line closed with 18 ...fxg6 19 hxg6 h6 looks fragile. White will be on the look out to make a timely sacrifice with Bxh6, tearing away the defensive pawn cover of the black king.

19 Rdg1 Ba8
20 Bg5 Be5
21 gxh7+ Kxh7

White should probably play 22 Be3 here, opening up the rook on the g-file and making sure the knight on d4 is always protected. His actual move is a mistake at the height of the tense battle.

22 Nb3?

22 ... Nxc2!
A serious blow. 23 Qxc2 Nxb3 is too bad for White, so he tries something else.

23 Nxc5 Na3+
Exploiting the pin on the b-pawn.

24 Ka2 Qxc5
25 Na4 Nc2!
A brilliant move. Can you see what happens if White captures the queen with 26 Nxc5?

26 Kb1 Qa3
Exploiting the pin on the b-pawn (again) and threatening b2 and a4. Now 27 Qxc2 Rfc8 28 Qd2 Qxa4 leaves Black with an easily winning attack, so Adams resigned. **0-1**

The Spanish Game

The Spanish Game is also known as the Ruy Lopez, after a 16th century Spanish priest who played the opening. It is easily White's most popular and effective way to continue after 1 e4 e5. The basic position arises after the further moves 2 Nf3 Nc6 3 Bb5.

White's development is quick and easy and he enjoys a variety of different possible middlegame plans. He can construct a strong pawn centre with c3 and d4 or play a quieter system with c3 and d3. Usually the main idea is to attack Black on the kingside. The white bishop on b5 will reroute to either b3 or c2, where it will be pointing at Black's castled king, and the queen's knight can head for the kingside via d2, f1 and g3, when it will be ready to spring forward to either f5 or h5. The plans are often long-term and both players will require a good deal of focus and concentration to avoid slipping into an inferior position.

The opening has been known since the 1400s and over the years has accumulated a large amount of theory. From the diagram above, Black has tried many third moves, including: 3 ...a6, 3 ...d6, 3 ...Nd4, 3 ...Bc5, 3 ...f5, 3 ...g6, 3 Nge7 and 3 ...Nf6. Even more obscure moves such as 3 ...Bb4, 3 ...Qf6 and 3 ...g5 have all been played. The most popular choices are 3 ...a6 and 3 ...Nf6.

It is important to note that after 1 e4 e5 2 Nf3 Nc6 3 Bb5 a6 4 Bxc6 dxc6 White cannot simply win a pawn with 5 Nxe5 because Black wins it back straight away with 5 ...Qd4, forking the knight and the e-pawn. 5 ...Qg5 is another way of achieving the same thing.

After 6 Nf3 Qxe4+ Black has an easy game.

Bobby Fischer – Hero of the Spanish Game

Bobby Fischer had great faith in the Spanish Game. He played it throughout his chess career and used it to win many fine games, including those against Boris Spassky in their famous World Championship match. The next two champions after Fischer – Anatoly Karpov and Garry Kasparov – also used the Spanish Game as a principal weapon in their king's pawn repertoires.

Bobby Fischer vs. Svetozar Gligoric
Rovinj/Zagreb, 1970

1 e4 e5	7 Bb3 d6
2 Nf3 Nc6	8 c3 0-0
3 Bb5 a6	9 h3 h6
4 Ba4 Nf6	10 d4 Re8
5 0-0 Be7	11 Nbd2 Bf8
6 Re1 b5	

A standard Spanish position. Gligoric was a great expert on the black side of this opening, so this game was of significance to opening theory. Fischer now reroutes his queen's knight to the kingside where he intends to launch an attack. Meanwhile, Gligoric completes his development by moving his queen's bishop to a good diagonal.

12 Nf1 Bb7
13 Ng3 Na5

Black's knight does a little dance to find a more effective square and also to allow his c7-pawn to challenge the white centre. The immediate intention to is exchange the knight for the bishop, which would be favourable for Black. White needs this bishop to support his kingside attack.

14 Bc2 Nc4
15 b3 Nb6
16 a4 c5
17 d5 c4

There is pressure all over the board and both players need to constantly take into account their opponent's intentions before continuing with their own plans. Fischer decides to block up the queenside before building up his kingside attack.

18 b4 Bc8
19 Be3 Bd7
20 a5 Nc8
21 Qd2 Nh7
22 Kh2 Be7
23 Nf5 Bg5

As further evidence of the extreme tension in the position, it should be noted that the next move is the first capture of the game.

24 Nxg5 hxg5
25 g4 g6
26 Ng3 f6

It takes great patience to play the Spanish Game successfully. It is not easy to come up with an attacking plan in this crowded position – but Fischer finds a way. He intends to play h3-h4 to open a file against Black's king. But first he needs to place a rook on the h-file and then move his king away before finally pushing the pawn.

27 Rh1 Rf8
28 Kg2 Rf7
29 f3 Nf8
30 h4 gxh4
31 Rxh4 Rh7

Black has defended well and his rook reaches the h-file just in time to oppose Fischer's rook. However, Fischer's second rook is ready to replace the first one. Gligoric's queen's rook is too far away from the action to help with the defence.

32 Rah1 Rxh4
33 Rxh4 g5?

Black finally cracks under the pressure. When under direct attack, it can be risky to move pawns in front of your king, as this will then create weaknesses. Of course, pawns cannot retreat to cover these weak squares.

34 Rh6 Kg7 35 Rxf6!

A fabulous and devastating rook sacrifice. If 35 ... Kxf6 then 36 Bxg5+ is a winning skewer and 35 ... Qxf6 loses the queen to the knight fork 36 Nh5+, so Gligoric resigned. **1-0**

Gligoric had already lost to Fischer's Spanish Opening in an earlier game, which saw an unusual variation.

Bobby Fischer vs. Svetozar Gligoric

Chess Olympiad, Havana, 1966

1 e4 e5
2 Nf3 Nc6
3 Bb5 a6
4 Bxc6

The Exchange Variation had long been thought harmless but several great Fischer games forced people to think again. In this line, White gives up his white-squared bishop – normally one of his favourite pieces – for a black knight. The basic idea behind this unexpected exchange is to give Black a set of doubled pawns. White is then quite prepared to swap off every other piece and head for an advantageous endgame.

Analysis diagram

This is the endgame White is aiming for. He has four kingside pawns against Black's three (a pawn majority) and that means if he advances with care – and a lot of help from the king – then he will eventually force one of the pawns through and promote it to a new queen. Black's pawn majority on the queenside isn't anywhere near as effective because one of the pawns is doubled. Under these circumstances, he will not usually be able to create and promote a passed pawn.

Naturally, a player as strong as Gligoric knows what is in store if he blindly allows White's plan to gradually unfold. So he tries a different approach,

trying to keep the game complicated and steering clear of the endgame.

4 ...dxc6
5 0-0 f6
6 d4 Bg4
7 c3 exd4
8 cxd4 Qd7
9 h3 Be6
10 Nc3 0-0-0

This is a dynamic position with chances for both sides. Every time players castle on opposite sides of the board they must think about launching an attack on the opponent's king as quickly as possible. Fischer and Gligoric now set about preparing their respective attacks.

11 Bf4 Ne7   15 fxg3 Kb8
12 Rc1 Ng6   16 Nc5 Qd6
13 Bg3 Bd6   17 Qa4
14 Na4 Bxg3

White's attack is a faster than Black's. Gligoric, under pressure, now makes a big mistake.

17 ...Ka7??
18 Nxa6!
Fischer's sacrifice is very strong and leads to a winning position. Incidentally, unlike some players – such as Tal – Fischer tended to sacrifice material only when he felt it to be the best move. He didn't like speculative moves but preferred to keep the game firmly under control.

18 ...Bxh3
Trying to drum up some urgent counterplay. The problem is that capturing the knight with 18 ...bxa6 loses quickly to 19 Rxc6, forking the black queen and the pawn on a6. After that, a possible line goes 19 ...Qxg3 20 Rxa6+ Kb7 21 Qb5+ Kc8 22 Ra8 checkmate. Gligoric is hoping that Fischer will now play 18 gxh3, allowing 18 ...Qxg3+ 19 Kh1 bxa6 20 Rxc6 Qxh3+ 21 Nh2 Qd3! when the black queen has miraculously found a way to protect the key a6 square. Fischer is quick to stamp out the counterplay.

19 e5 Nxe5
Gligoric continues to try to confuse the issue, which is really the only thing he can do.

20 dxe5 fxe5
21 Nc5+ Kb8
22 gxh3 e4
23 Nxe4 Qe7
24 Rc3 b5
25 Qc2
Black is two knights down and has no hope of fighting back, so he resigned. **1-0**

Bobby Fischer vs. Boris Spassky
World Championship Rematch, Belgrade, 1992

After he defeated Boris Spassky to become World Champion in 1972, Bobby Fischer gave up competitive chess for 20 years. He returned to the board for just one more match (against Spassky again). This was in 1992 and it made front page headlines around the world. For his first comeback game he remained true to his favourite white opening.

1 e4 e5	6 Re1 b5
2 Nf3 Nc6	7 Bb3 d6
3 Bb5 a6	8 c3 0-0
4 Ba4 Nf6	9 h3 Nb8
5 0-0 Be7	

Black's chosen line is known as the Breyer Defence, which Spassky frequently employed. It looks odd to retreat the knight, but Black is merely relocating it to a more effective square.

10 d4 Nbd7
11 Nbd2 Bb7
12 Bc2 Re8
13 Nf1 Bf8
14 Ng3 g6

Fischer was a great expert in this type of position. He is limbering up for a kingside attack but this will only be launched after thorough preparation.

15 Bg5 h6
16 Bd2 Bg7
17 a4 c5
Correctly challenging the centre.

18 d5 c4
19 b4 Nh7
20 Be3 h5
21 Qd2 Rf8
Spassky has set up a solid position on the kingside and can safely repulse any direct attack in that area - so Fischer decides to probe on the queenside.

22 Ra3 Ndf6
23 Rea1 Qd7
24 R1a2 Rfc8
25 Qc1 Bf8
26 Qa1 Qe8
27 Nf1 Be7
28 N1d2 Kg7
29 Nb1

A remarkable position. Fischer appears to be ready to break open the queenside and it concerns Spassky so much that he decides to sacrifice material to change the course of the game.

29 ...Nxe4
The first capture of the game! If Spassky can destroy the white centre and push his extra pawns down the board, then he will gain good counterplay for the sacrificed knight.

30 Bxe4 f5
31 Bc2 Bxd5
32 axb5 axb5
33 Ra7 Kf6
34 Nbd2 Rxa7
35 Rxa7 Ra8
36 g4

There is action all over the board. Fischer, who already has a solid grip on the queenside, is now gunning for Spassky's king.

36 ...hxg4
37 hxg4 Rxa7
38 Qxa7 f4

If the bishop runs away with 39 Bb6 then Black's king will feel more secure. Fischer finds a more direct approach: he will sacrifice his bishop to strip away some of the strong black pawns.

39 Bxf4 exf4
40 Nh4 Bf7
41 Qd4+ Ke6
42 Nf5!
An excellent way to bring the knight straight back into the game. Now if 42 ...gxf5 then 43 Bxf5 is checkmate.

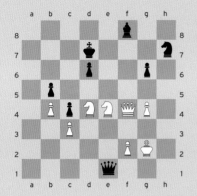

42 ... Bf8
43 Qxf4 Kd7
44 Nd4 Qe1+
45 Kg2 Bd5+
46 Be4 Bxe4+
47 Nxe4

White's centralized pieces give him a big advantage. Black's pieces are uncoordinated and cannot work as a team. Fischer finishes the game in ruthless style.

47 ...Be7
48 Nxb5 Nf8
49 Nbxd6 Ne6
50 Qe5

A famous final position. Fischer's threat is to checkmate in three moves: 51 Qb5+ Kd8 52 Qb8+ Kd7 53 Qc8 mate. Black has an alternative line but it doesn't last any longer. 51 Qb5+ Kc7 52 Qb7+ Kd8 53 Qc8 checkmate. 50 ...Bxd6 eliminates one of the attacking knights but at the cost of two pieces: 51 Qxd6+ and 52 Qxe6+. Apart from the checkmates, White is also threatening 51 Nc5+ and 51 Nf6+, followed by 52 Qxe1. So Spassky resigned. **1-0**

The Catalan Opening

The Catalan Opening is a very good alternative for White to a traditional Queen's Gambit. It suffered from a drawish reputation for some years but has become a much more popular opening over the last decade or so.

After **1 d4 d5 2 c4 e6**, White opts for **3 g3** (or sometimes **3 Nf3** and then **4 g3**).

White clearly intends to develop his king's bishop on g2 (a fianchetto). It will then exert great pressure along the h1-a8 diagonal. As in the normal Queen's Gambit, after an exchange of pawns it is very likely that the c-file will be opened, allowing White's rooks to add to the queenside pressure.

Catalan games rarely end in quick victories, for either colour. Both players need to keep their positional skills up to the mark to maintain the balance and Black must closely observe the activity of White's Catalan bishop.

Vladimir Kramnik - Hero of the Catalan Opening

Vladimir Kramnik's style of play is very positional. He is capable of grinding out very long endgame wins, very much in the style of Tigran Petrosian. But Kramnik is also a deadly tactician and far more prepared to 'mix it' than was Petrosian.

Kramnik is the one of the world's most consistent Catalan players and he has used the opening at the very highest levels of match and tournament chess.

1 d4 Nf6
2 c4 e6
3 g3 d5
4 Bg2 Be7
5 Nf3 0-0
6 0-0 dxc4
7 Qc2 a6

Black can try to defend the pawn but it is too risky. 7 ...b5 8 a4 a6 9 axb5 leaves the a6-pawn pinned, so it won't be able to recapture on b5. The alternative 7 ...b5 8 a4 c6 also runs into big trouble after 9 axb5 cxb5 10 Ng5 and Black must lose material. Black's rook is under attack from the Catalan bishop and if he blocks the diagonal with 10 Nd5 then 11 Qxh7 is checkmate.

8 Qxc4 b5
9 Qc2 Bb7

This is the main line of the Catalan Opening. White hopes to exert considerable pressure on the c-file and the h1-a8 diagonal. If Black can successfully advance his c-pawn to c5 he will have a good position.

10 Bd2

The plan is to play 11 Ba5, pinning the c-pawn, and then follow up by applying as much pressure as possible to the c7 square.

10 ...Be4
11 Qc1 Qc8

Black is now ready to meet 12 Ba5? with 12 ...Nc6 and if the bishop retreats Black can win a pawn with 13 ...Bxf3 and 14 ...Nxd4, so White relocates his bishop to another square.

Vladimir Kramnik vs. Peter Leko
World Championship, Mexico City, 2007

12 Bg5 Nbd7	16 Bxf6 Nxf6
13 Qf4 Bb7	17 Nbd2 Re8
14 Rc1 Bd6	18 e4 Nd7
15 Qh4 h6	

Kramnik's big centre gives him a slight advantage but Leko has well developed pieces and a solid position.

19 Nb3 a5
20 Nc5 Be7
21 Qf4

The pressure on c7 is making itself felt again. White's threat is 22 Nxd7 Qxd7 23 Rxc7, with a winning position. Leko is prompted to take action in the centre.

21 ...e5
22 Nxe5 Nxe5
23 dxe5 Bg5

A pin that wins the exchange (a rook for a bishop). However, Kramnik has plenty of compensation.

24 Qf3 Bxc1
25 Rxc1 Rxe5
26 Qc3

Black must tread very carefully. If his rook retreats then Kramnik gains a serious advantage: 26 ...Re7 27 Nxb7 Qxb7 28 e5 and the Catalan bishop will crash through and capture the rook on a8 (after Black's queen moves away). Leko plays to keep his extra material but he has to weaken his kingside. Kramnik is very quick to move into the weak white squares.

26 ...f6	30 Nf4 Rd6
27 Qb3+ Kh8	31 Ng6+ Kh7
28 Qf7 Bc6	32 e5!
29 Nd3 Re6	

The Catalan bishop is unleashed and Black will now lose material.

32 ...fxe5
33 Bxc6 Rf6

33 ...Rxg6? 34 Be4! with a pin on the rook was not acceptable to Black.

34 Qd5 Qf5
35 Bxa8 Qxf2+

It looks dangerous to allow Black to invade the white king's position, but Kramnik is confident that there is no real danger after the initial check. Once the smoke clears he will still be a piece ahead.

36 Kh1 Qxb2
37 Qc5 Kxg6
38 Be4+ Kh5
39 Rb1

Leko does not have enough compensation for being a piece down, so he resigned.

1-0

Vladimir Kramnik vs. Magnus Carlsen
Dortmund, 2007

1 Nf3 Nf6	6 0-0 dxc4
2 c4 e6	7 Qc2 a6
3 g3 d5	8 Qxc4 b5
4 d4 Be7	9 Qc2 Bb7
5 Bg2 0-0	10 Bd2 Nc6

Preventing 11 Ba5.

11 e3 Nb4
12 Bxb4 Bxb4
13 a3 Be7
14 Nbd2 Rc8
15 b4

Kramnik's plan is simple to understand. He aims to keep the black c-pawn pinned down on c7, while he generates more and more pressure against it. His pawns on b4 and d4 serve as a big clamp.

15 ...a5
16 Ne5
For once, Kramnik is happy to exchange his Catalan bishop - but Carlsen declines to oblige with 16 ...Bxg2. The problem is that the c6 square would then be left in a very weak condition, and Kramnik's knight will land there very quickly.

16 ...Nd5
17 Nb3 axb4
Carlsen is trying to distract Kramnik from his plan but it doesn't work. The c6 square will be occupied by a white knight after all.

18 Na5 Ba8
19 Nac6 Bxc6
20 Nxc6 Qd7
21 Bxd5 exd5
22 axb4 Rfe8
23 Ra5 Bf8
24 Ne5

Black is simply unable to defend his queenside pawns.

24 ...Qe6
25 Rxb5 Rb8
26 Rxb8 Rxb8
27 Qxc7 Bd6
28 Qa5 Bxb4

At first glance it appears that Carlsen has fought back to reduce his material deficit to a single pawn but, unfortunately for him, Kramnik has a winning pin.

29 Rb1! Qd6
 29 ...Bxa5 fails to 30 Rxb8+ with checkmate to follow.

30 Qa4
Black can avoid the loss of a full piece with 30 ...Bc3 but after 31 Rxb8+ Qxb8 32 Qd7 Qf8 33 Qxd5, White's advantage of two strong pawns is enough for victory. Carlsen resigned. **1-0**

Vladimir Kramnik vs. Alexander Morozevich

World Championship, Mexico City, 2007

1 Nf3 Nf6

Playing 1 d4 is not the only way to enter a Catalan. The game soon transposes to a position usually reached by a more conventional move-order.

2 c4 e6   4 d4 dxc4
3 g3 d5   5 Bg2 a6

Morozevich prefers sharp and complicated positions to those of a quiet nature, so he aims to steer clear of the main lines and hopes to cause Kramnik some original problems. If Kramnik plays the typical Catalan move 6 Qc2, hoping to recapture the pawn, then Morozevich will try to hold on to it with 6 ...b5. Kramnik's next move unleashes his king's bishop, making ...b5 more difficult to achieve (6 ...b5 7 Bxa8).

6 Ne5 Bb4+   8 0-0
7 Nc3 Nd5

Kramnik offers a pawn sacrifice. After 8 ...Nxc3 9 bxc3 Bxc3 10 Rb1 Qxd4 11 Qxd4 Bxd4 12 Nxc4, Black is ahead in material but White's active pieces and immense pressure on the queenside would make it very difficult for him to complete his development. Morozevich is not as happy defending as he is attacking, so he declined Kramnik's sacrifice.

8 ...0-0
9 Qc2 b5
10 Nxd5 exd5
11 b3

Black's queenside pawns control a lot of space. If they can remain intact then he will have an advantage. Kramnik must try to break them up before they can stabilize. The immediate threat is 12 bxc4 bxc4 13 Nxc4, exploiting the pin on the d-pawn (13 ...dxc4 14 Bxa8).

11 ...c6
12 e4 f6

An important moment in the game. Kramnik leaves his knight where it is. Morozevich accepts the sacrifice, but at the cost of seeing his pawn structure shattered.

13 exd5 fxe5
14 bxc4 exd4
15 dxc6 Be6

Kramnik could win back the sacrificed material here with 16 c7 Qxc7 17 Bxa8 but first he continues his plan of demolishing the black pawn structure.

16 cxb5 d3
17 c7

This is a very unusual case of both queens being under attack by pawns. The simplifying variation 17 ...dxc2 18 cxd8=Q Rxd8 19 Bxa8 is better for White, so Morozevich keeps the complications alive.

17 ...Qd4
18 Qa4 Nd7

18 ...Qxa1 19 Qxb4 is much better for White as he is still going to win either the knight or rook in the corner.

19 Be3
Protecting his rook and attacking the queen before capturing the rook.

19 ...Qd6
20 Bxa8 Rxa8
21 Bf4 Qf8
22 b6! Ne5
22 ...Nxb6 runs into a fork with 23 Qc6, attacking the knight and the bishop. With two connected passed pawns so close to queening, things are looking excellent for Kramnik. Morozevich has one last chance - to attack Kramnik's king on the weakened white squares.

23 Bxe5 Qf3

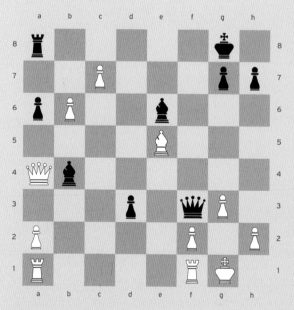

Morozevich will force checkmate on g2 if he can safely play 24 ...Bd5 or 24 ...Bh3, but Kramnik is fully alert to the danger.

24 Qd1 Qe4
25 b7 Rf8
26 c8=Q Bd5
27 f3

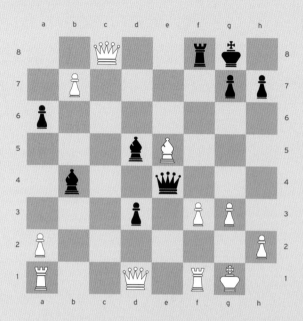

With two queens on the board, Kramnik can afford to leave the bishop to be captured on e5 by the black queen. With his checkmate plans thwarted, Morozevich is left with too great a material deficit to fight on any longer.

1-0

The Nimzo-Indian Defence

The peculiar name of this defence is taken from two sources. 'Nimzo' is a shortened version of the name of Aron Nimzowitsch, who was one of the strongest players in the world in the days of Capablanca and Alekhine. He was noted for his very creative – and often very unusual – chess ideas. The second part of the name of the opening refers to the old Indian form of chess, where pawns did not have the option of moving more than one square on their initial move. There are a number of other Indian defences against the queen's pawn openings, including the Queen's Indian, Bogo-Indian (named after Efim Bogoljubow, an unsuccessful challenger for the World Championship title in 1929 and 1934) and King's Indian.

The basic position arises after the moves **1 d4 Nf6 2 c4 e6 3 Nc3 Bb4**.

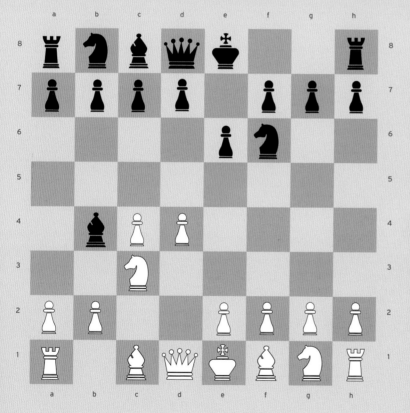

Black's pin on the c3 knight is part of a major battle for the control of the centre. If, for example, Black had played 3 ...Be7, then White would immediately seize control of the board with 4 e4! and Black would face a struggle to gain any meaningful play. After 3 ...Bb4, the stubborn 4 e4?? just loses a pawn to 4 ...Nxe4. White has several different respectable lines against the Nimzo-Indian. 4 Qc2 and 4 e3 are currently the most popular options.

Black is hoping for a positional game. One of his principal ideas is to exchange his bishop for the knight on c3, leaving White with a compromised pawn structure. The doubled pawns on the c-file and the isolated pawn on a3 could become very weak in the endgame. After the exchange, Black will usually try to keep the position closed, so as to prevent White's bishop pair from being unleashed.

Anatoly Karpov – Hero of the Nimzo-Indian Defence

Anatoly Karpov was not only a mighty champion; he also accumulated a fantastic tournament record – winning more first prizes than any other world title holder. At the height of his powers he was almost impossible to stop when he had the white pieces and an extremely tough nut to crack when he played the black side. The Nimzo-Indian Defence suited his style and it was an important part of his repertoire during his epic battles for the World Championship.

1 d4 Nf6
2 c4 e6
3 Nc3 Bb4
4 Bg5

This is the Leningrad System. It was a favourite weapon of Boris Spassky. It avoids the longer variations of main line theory and aims to set the opponent more unusual problems.

4 ...h6
5 Bh4 c5
6 d5 d6
7 e3 Bxc3+

Karpov takes the opportunity to double White's pawns, which is a standard theme in the Nimzo-Indian. These pawns may prove to be very weak later in the game. However, the plan comes at a cost, as Karpov has to give up his dark-squared bishop for a knight. If Williams can open up the game, his bishop pair could be very powerful, so Karpov spends the next few moves closing the position and keeping the bishops hemmed in behind pawns.

Howard Williams vs. Anatoly Karpov
Olympiad, Nice, 1974

8 bxc3 e5
9 Bd3 e4
10 Bc2 g5
11 Bg3 Qe7

White is in danger of being completely outplayed, so he rightly attempts to open up the position.

12 h4 Rg8
13 hxg5 hxg5
14 Ne2 Nbd7
15 Qb1

15 ...Kd8
16 a4 a5
17 Ra2 Kc7
18 Rh6 Ra6
19 Qb5 Kb8
20 Rb2 Ka7

The job is done. Black's position is rock-solid and he can take his time targeting White's pawn weaknesses. White's advanced pieces are only apparently aggressive as they have nothing to attack; indeed, they are soon forced back into their own half of the board.

21 Qb3 Ng4	25 Qxb2 b6
22 Rh1 f5	26 Bb3 Ba6
23 Kd1 Rb6	27 Nc1 Nde5
24 Qa2 Rxb2	

Karpov needs a plan to ensure the completion of his development. The conventional route would involve moving his queen's knight again to release his queenside pieces, but 15 ...Nb6 is a little clumsy as it leaves the knight misplaced. After 16 a4 the tempting 16 ...Nxc4?? is a blunder, due to the fork 17 Qb5+, winning the knight. 15 ... Ne5 leads to an exchange of pawns after 16 Bxe4 Nxc4, but the white bishops will enjoy the greater freedom once the e4-pawn has gone. Finally, 15 ... Nf8 runs into 16 Qb5+ which is uncomfortable for Black because interposing with 16 ...Bd7 allows 17 Qxb7 and 16 ...Qd7 fails to 17 Bxd6! winning a key pawn, thanks to the pin on the queen which makes 17 ...Qxd6 impossible.

Karpov takes a more unconventional route, spending the next few moves safeguarding his king and developing his queen's rook via an unusual route. He is only able to do this because the position is closed and White cannot exploit the slowness of the plan.

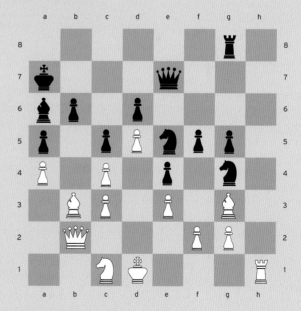

Karpov has succeeded in dominating the position. The pressure on the weak c4-pawn is absolutely typical of the Nimzo-Indian Defence.

28 Qe2 Ng6
29 Kd2 Nf6
30 Qd1 f4

Mark Taimanov vs. Anatoly Karpov
Moscow, 1973

1 d4 Nf6	4 e3 c5	7 0-0 dxc4
2 c4 e6	5 Bd3 0-0	8 Bxc4 cxd4
3 Nc3 Bb4	6 Nf3 d5	9 exd4 b6

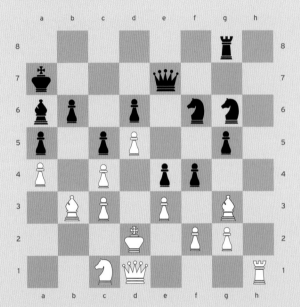

Karpov has a big advantage. Williams has two ways to react to the threat to his bishop, but neither is convincing. 31 Bh2 Ne5 threatens the c4-pawn again and if White protects it with his queen – by 32 Qe2 or 32 Qf1 – then Black can play 32 ...Nxd5, exploiting the pin by the bishop on the c4-pawn. The alternative 31 exf4 isn't any better. After 31 ...gxf4 32 Bh2 e3+ White is powerless to defend his king, now that the floodgates have opened. So White resigned.

0-1

Once again Karpov has inflicted a potential pawn weakness on the white position. The isolated queen's pawn will be difficult to defend in an endgame. Meanwhile, Taimanov must use his superior control of space wisely in order to drum up attacking chances.

10 Qe2 Bb7
11 Rd1 Nbd7
12 Bd2 Rc8

Now Taimanov should probably retreat his bishop with 13 Bd3, to ensure it is adequately protected. With the move he actually plays in the game, he allows Karpov to trade a couple of minor pieces, making the game less complicated and bringing the endgame a step closer. On the other hand, by changing the pawn structure White secures additional protection for his d-pawn.

13 Ba6 Bxa6
14 Qxa6 Bxc3
15 bxc3 Rc7
16 Rac1 Qc8
17 Qa4

White's c- and d-pawns are known as hanging pawns. They are at their strongest when they sit side by side, controlling a batch of squares in front of them. White will stand well if he can safely advance his c-pawn to c4. Karpov finds an interesting and creative way of keeping the pawns in their current positions, where they make the white bishop on d2 look rather clumsy and lacking in scope.

17 ...Rc4
A pawn sacrifice.

18 Qxa7 Qc6
Threatening to trap the white queen with 18 ... Ra8.

19 Qa3 Rc8
20 h3 h6
In return for the sacrificed pawn, Karpov has great piece coordination and long-term pressure on White's queenside pawns.

21 Rb1 Ra4
22 Qb3 Nd5
23 Rdc1 Rc4
24 Rb2 f6

It was possible simply to capture the pawn here with 24 ...Nxc3, when the position burns itself out to drawish equality after 25 Rxc3 Rxc3 26 Bxc3 Qxc3 27 Qxc3 Rxc3. With 24 ...f6, Karpov is quietly improving the position of his king - in anticipation of the endgame - and revealing that he is playing for a win.

25 Re1 Kf7
26 Qd1 Nf8
27 Rb3 Ng6
28 Qb1 Ra8
29 Re4 Rca4
30 Rb2 Nf8
31 Qd3

A clever move by White. Most players with the black pieces would be tempted to capture the pawn with 31 ...Rxa2, but after 32 Rxa2 Rxa2 White finally gets his hanging pawns moving by 33 c4!, with advantage. Karpov is not tempted by the bait and keeps the pawns under lock and key. Karpov's great patience was always one of his greatest strengths. His opponents would frequently run short of time on the chess clock and crack under the pressure.

31 ...Rc4
32 Re1 Ra3
33 Qb1 Ng6
34 Rc1

A good position to demonstrate Karpov's positional mastery. Only now, after immense preparation, does he capture one of the queenside pawns he targeted so many moves ago.

34 ...Nxc3
35 Qd3 Ne2+!
Forcing an advantageous simplification.

36 Qxe2 Rxc1+
37 Bxc1 Qxc1+
38 Kh2

Taimanov had almost run out of time at this point and Karpov switches from a positional squeeze to a speedy tactical finish.

38 ...Rxf3!
The most desirable capture - 39 Qxf3 - fails to 39 ...Qxb2, as the white queen has been deflected. There just remains the capture by the pawn, but then the white king is left severely weakened.

39 gxf3 Nh4
Taimanov lost on time here. This is a very difficult position to defend, as the following options reveal:
a) 40 Rc2 Qf4+ 41 Kh1 Nxf3 (threatening 42 ... Qh2 checkmate) 42 Kg2 Nxd4 43 Qe3 Qd6 44 Rd2 e5 and Black, with his much safer king and a powerful knight and two extra pawns against White's rook, has a solid advantage.
b) 40 Rb3 Qg5 (threatening checkmate again; note the fine coordination of the queen and knight which are now making all of Black's moves) 41 Qf1 Qf4+ and 42 ...Nxf3 with a winning attack for Black.
c) 40 Rxb6?? Qc7+ is a winning fork.
0-1

Lajos Portisch vs. Anatoly Karpov
Bugojno, 1978

1 d4 Nf6
2 c4 e6
3 Nc3 Bb4
4 e3 0-0
5 Bd3 c5
6 Nf3 d5
7 0-0 dxc4
8 Bxc4 cxd4
9 exd4 b6

Reaching the same position as in the Taimanov game. Portisch tries a different tenth move.

10 Bg5 Bb7
11 Re1 Nbd7
12 Rc1 Rc8
13 Bd3 Bxc3
14 bxc3 Qc7
15 c4 Rfe8

Karpov has been unable to keep White's c-pawn pinned down on c3 and Portisch's hanging pawns are looking powerful. Black needs a different plan this time.

16 Qe2 h6
17 Bd2 Bxf3

At first glance this seems a very surprising decision. Black trades his excellent bishop and leaves White with two bishops vs. two knights, which might soon represent a big advantage. However, it is an essential part of Karpov's plan, which involves attacking the hanging pawns in a very direct manner. The white knight controls the important e5 square, which Karpov is hoping to exploit to his advantage.

18 Qxf3 e5

White needs to be careful to avoid ending up with very weak pawns. For example, 19 dxe5 Nxe5 leaves the a- and c-pawns in a bad way. 19 d5 gives White a passed pawn but loses control of the c5-square; Black will then play 19 ...Nc5 and follow up with 20 ...e4, gaining space and annoying the white pieces.

19 Qg3

A pawn sacrifice. Portisch is hoping to open up the game to give his bishops more scope. The immediate threat is 20 Bxh6 (exploiting the pin on the g-pawn).

19 ...exd4
20 Bxh6 would now fail to 20 ...Qxg3 21 hxg3 gxh6.

20 Rxe8+ Nxe8
21 Bf4 Qc6
22 Bf5 Rd8
23 h3 Nc5
24 Rd1

At first sight, Portisch's position looks good, with his queen and two bishops directed at the black king. However, Karpov's game is very solid indeed and there is no obvious way for White to create a serious attack. Karpov's next few moves are very powerful. He forces away one of the attackers, picks up one of the weak pawns, safeguards his king against the threat of Bxh6, and strengthens his grip on the centre. It sounds so simple, yet Portisch was one of the strongest players in the world at the time of this game and he was very difficult to beat. It shows just how powerful Karpov was in his prime; his best games display an almost effortless quality that allowed him to crack even the toughest of nuts.

24 ...Qf6	**27 Be5 Qxc4**	**30 Qe2 Nd6**
25 Bb1 Qe6	**28 Qf4 Ne6**	**31 a4 Nc4**
26 Kh2 Kf8	**29 Qe4 Qd5**	**32 Bg3 Nc5**

Black's dominance is clear. He is winning both positionally and materially.

33 Ba2 d3
34 Qe1 Qd4
35 f3 Ne3
36 Rd2 Re8
37 Qc1 Nxa4
Completing his raid on all of White's queenside pawns.

38 Kh1 Nc5
39 Bf2 Qe5
40 Bb1 Kg8
White's position is absolutely hopeless and 41 Bxd3 runs into 41 ...Nb3 with a terrible fork, so he chose this moment to resign. **0-1**

The Queen's Gambit

1 d4 d5 2 c4 is the Queen's Gambit.

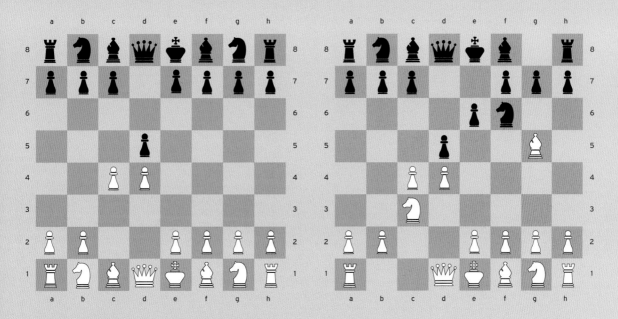

White is offering a temporary pawn sacrifice to try to tempt Black into giving up the centre. After 2 ...dxc4 (the Queen's Gambit Accepted) White can either rush to occupy the centre with his pawns – 3 e4 – or develop more methodically and occupy it a little later (3 Nf3, 4 e3, 5 Bxc4, 6 0-0 followed shortly by e3-e4). There is nothing wrong with playing the black side of the Queen's Gambit Accepted but some players feel uncomfortable allowing their opponents an obvious advantage in space.

Therefore, from the diagram, the most popular and solid reply is **2 ...e6** (the Queen's Gambit Declined). The next few moves are all about exerting pressure on the centre of the board. **3 Nc3 Nf6 4 Bg5**

This is the basic position for the Queen's Gambit Declined, although 4 cxd5 – the Exchange Variation – is another very good option. From the diagram, White will continue to develop and build up a very solid position, particularly in the centre of the board. It is highly likely that his c- pawn will be traded for Black's d-pawn at some stage and this will give him a half-open c-file for his rooks and queen. Black may suffer a cramped position for a while, as it is more difficult for him to develop his pieces quickly. His queen's bishop is in particular danger of ending up sitting passively for a long time.

Alexander Alekhine - Hero of the Queen's Gambit

Alexander Alekhine was equally at home with 1 e4 and 1 d4. However, it was the move 1 d4 that helped him win his titanic 1927 World Championship match with the 'unbeatable' Capablanca. One of Alekhine's greatest strengths was his ability to whip up incredibly dangerous attacks with which he would - more often than not - simply blow his opponents off the board. The Queen's Gambit enabled him to achieve a very sound position for his forces before he launched his trademark attacks, as our illustrative games will show.

1 d4 Nf6

Black doesn't have to employ the traditional move-order with 1 ...d5. After the third move, the game transposes straight back into a Queen's Gambit Declined.

2 c4 e6

Alexander Alekhine vs. Walter Michel
Bern, 1925

3 Nc3 d5
4 Bg5 Nbd7

Black sets a little trap. It looks like White can win a pawn here with 5 cxd5 exd5 6 Nxd5, but the trap is revealed after the unexpected reply 6 ...Nxd5! when 7 Bxd8 Bb4+ forces 8 Qd2 Bxd2+ 9 Kxd2 Kxd8 leaving Black a piece up.

5 e3 Be7
6 Nf3 c6
7 Bd3 0-0
8 0-0 a6
9 a4 h6
10 Bh4 dxc4
11 Bxc4 Nd5

Black offers to exchange two sets of minor pieces. 12 Bxe7 Qxe7 13 Nxd5 exd5 would free Black's position considerably and, in addition, will strengthen his centre and provide his queen's bishop with an easy route into the game (as it will no longer be blocked by a pawn on e6). Alekhine prefers to keep things as complicated as possible. He is happy enough to allow Black to play ...Nxc3 at some point as his own pawn centre will be strengthened after bxc3, but he is not prepared to allow a trade of bishops.

12 Bg3 a5

A standard device to lock down the white queenside pawns. Michel is eyeing the weak b4 square, which he will use as an outpost for one of his knights.

13 Qe2 Nb4
14 Rad1 Nf6
15 Ne5 Qb6

Black's position is still cramped and he has yet to solve the problem of how best to develop his queen's bishop. Alekhine's pieces are nicely developed. With everything in place, he now decides to start an attack.

16 e4 Rd8

Attacking the d-pawn.

17 Bf4!

Defending the pawn indirectly. 17 ...Rxd4 runs into the pin 18 Be3, when Black will lose his rook for the white bishop. Alekhine also has a second, deeper idea in mind for the bishop. He wants to use his f-pawn to attack the black king and therefore relocates his bishop so it will complement and not impede this kingside advance.

17 ... Bd7
18 Bd2

18 Bc1 was another way to do the same thing, but Alekhine decides to set a little trap.

18 ...Qc7

18 ...Qxd4 19 Nxd7 was Alekhine's idea. Then, regardless of how he captures the knight, thanks to the discovered attack on the black queen, he can play 20 Bxh6 stripping away part of the enemy king's defensive wall,

19 f4 Be8
20 f5

A typical Alekhine attack. The f-pawn acts as a battering ram as it endeavours to smash open lines to the black king. Both the bishop on c4 and the rook on f1 see their power increase as obstacles are removed from their paths.

20 ...exf5
21 Rxf5 Bf8

White has several good moves here, including 22 Bxh6, a temporary sacrifice to remove the guard of the knight (22 ...gxh6 23 Rxf6). Alekhine prefers to increase the pressure a little more before launching the decisive phase of his attack.

22 Rdf1 Rd6
23 Ng4 Rd7

Black cracks under the pressure. He had to try 23 ...Nxg4, in order to eliminate one of the attacking pieces, although he would still have found it very difficult to defend the position for much longer.

24 Rxf6! gxf6
25 Nxf6+

Black has two possible moves but they both lead to checkmate: 25 ...Kg7 26 Qg4+ Kh8 27 Qg8 checkmate and 25 ...Kh8 26 Qg4 Bg7 27 Bxh6! Bxf6 28 Rxf6 with checkmate to follow on g7. Black resigned. **1-0**

Alexander Alekhine vs. Frederick Yates
London, 1922

1 d4 Nf6
2 c4 e6

An interesting move-order. If White continues with 3 Nc3 then Black has the option of playing the Nimzo-Indian Defence. Here Alekhine decides to avoid that defence and the game transposes to a Queen's Gambit as soon as Black plays 3 d5.

3 Nf3 d5

Other options at this point are 3 ...b6 (the Queen's Indian Defence); 3 ...Bb4+ (the Bogo-Indian Defence) and 3 ...c5 (the Modern Benoni Defence).

4 Nc3 Be7
5 Bg5 0-0
6 e3 Nbd7

There now begins a small sequence designed to gain a move (known as a battle for tempo). White wants to play Bd3 at some point but if he does it now then Black will reply with 7 ...dxc4, essentially forcing the bishop to waste a move because of having to recapture immediately with 8 Bxc4. Ideally, White would like to defer any move of his king's bishop until Black plays ...dxc4, so he can he recapture the pawn and develop his bishop in one move with Bxc4. Therefore both players proceed with a couple of other standard developing moves before one side gives up the battle for tempo.

7 Rc1 c6
8 Qc2 Re8

White has run out of normal moves and must now develop his bishop, whereupon Black duly replies with the expected capture.

9 Bd3 dxc4
10 Bxc4 Nd5

Yates wants to exchange some pieces to free up his position; an idea familiar from Alekhine's game with Michel. Here, Alekhine's bishop is on g5 instead of h4, so he cannot avoid the bishop exchange. Therefore he strives to keep the game complicated by ensuring the knights remain on the board.

11 Ne4 f5?!

A risky move, especially against Alekhine. Yates attacks the centralized knight but weakens his own king's defence. He should have played 11 ... Qa5+, exploiting the fact that Alekhine hasn't yet castled. Alekhine would then have had the choice of interposing with 12 Qd2 (allowing an exchange of queens, which wouldn't have pleased him), 12 Kf1 (giving up the right to castle, which can't be a good idea) or retreating with one of his knights to block the check (which leads to complications which may be slightly in Black's favour; for example, 11 ...Qa5+ 12 Nec3 Nb4! attacking the queen and also discovering an attack by the black queen on the bishop on g5).

12 Bxe7 Qxe7
13 Ned2 b5
14 Bxd5 cxd5
15 0-0

Yates has managed to exchange some pieces and stabilize the centre. The structure of pawns on d5, e6 and f5 is known as a Stonewall formation. It can be difficult to break down but Alekhine has two advantages in this position: he has total control of the open c-file and Black's bishop is a very poor piece as it is hemmed in by its own pawns.

15	...a5	19	Rxc5 b4
16	Nb3 a4	20	Rfc1 Ba6
17	Nc5 Nxc5	21	Ne5 Reb8
18	Qxc5 Qxc5		

Material is equal but Yates has major problems of a positional nature. He can never chase the knight out of the e5 hole and he is going to struggle to prevent an invasion by White's rooks along the c-file. Alekhine's plan is fairly simple. He is going to ensure that all of his pieces – including his king – are in ideal positions and then he will strike a killer blow. There's no hurry and White can take all the time he needs as Black can't generate any serious counterplay.

22 f3 b3	29 R5c6 Re8
23 a3 h6	30 Kf4 Kg8
24 Kf2 Kh7	31 h5 Bf1
25 h4 Rf8	32 g3 Ba6
26 Kg3 Rfb8	33 Rf7 Kh7
27 Rc7 Bb5	34 Rcc7 Rg8
28 R1c5 Ba6	

An excellent example of positional domination. Everything is now in place for a decisive thrust, which Alekhine delivers with a little pirouette from his knight.

35 Nd7!
Threatening a terrible knight fork with 36 Nf6+, exploiting the pin on the g-pawn.

35 ...Kh8
36 Nf6 Rgf8
Black still couldn't capture the knight as 36 ....gxf6 allows 37 Rh7 checkmate.

37 Rxg7! Rxf6
38 Ke5

A fabulous finishing touch by the king. Black's rook is under attack and if it moves back to f8 then White checkmates the black king with 39 Rh7+ and 40 Rcg7 mate. Defending the rook with 38 ...Raf8 allows the same checkmate. Black is going to lose his rook and will be checkmated shortly afterwards, so he resigned. **1-0**

Alexander Alekhine vs. Ernst Grunfeld
Chess Olympiad, Prague, 1931

1 d4 d5	3 c4 e6
2 Nf3 Nf6	4 Nc3 c5

This is the Semi-Tarrasch Defence. The Tarrasch Defence arises after 1 d4 d5 2 c4 e6 3 Nc3 c5 but some players don't like ending up with an isolated queen's pawn after 4 cxd5 exd5 and a further exchange of the c5-pawn. The Semi-Tarrasch allows Black to recapture on d5 with a knight, thereby retaining a more solid pawn structure.

5 cxd5 Nxd5	
6 e4 Nxc3	
7 bxc3 cxd4	
8 cxd4 Bb4+	
9 Bd2 Bxd2+	
10 Qxd2 0-0	

A standard Semi-Tarrasch position. White has more space and more pawns in the centre. Black has a queenside pawn majority, which will be useful if he can reach an endgame – as then he will be able to advance his a- and b-pawns and force one through against White's lone queenside pawn.

11 Be2 Nd7	
12 0-0 b6	
13 Rac1 Bb7	
14 Qf4 Nf6	
15 Bd3 Rc8	
16 Rxc8 Bxc8	
17 Rc1 Bb7	
18 h3 Re8	

Grunfeld's position looks very solid. His pieces are developed and he has managed to exchange one set of rooks, bishops and knights. Alekhine's pieces are also well placed and his centre is strong. As usual, once he has everything in place, he starts an attack at the first possible opportunity.

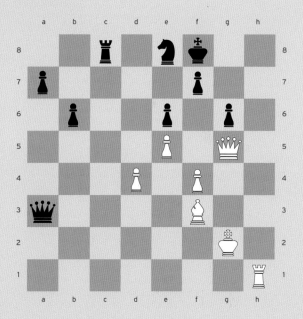

19 e5 Nh5
20 Qg4 Bxf3
21 Qxf3 g6
22 g4 Ng7
23 Bb5 Rf8
24 Qe3 h5
25 Be2 Qd5
26 a3 Rd8

Black seems to be holding the position, despite Alekhine's aggressive intentions. White's d-pawn is now under attack.

27 Bf3! Qd7
27 ...Qxd4 falls for a skewer by 28 Rd1, when Black will have to give up his queen for a rook and a bishop with 28 ...Qxd1+ 29 Bxd1 Rxd1+ 30 Kg2.

28 Qg5
Resuming the attack and threatening 28 gxh5 gxh5 29 Bxh5, exploiting the pin on the knight.

28 ...hxg4
29 hxg4 Rc8
A good defensive try. If he can swap off more pieces he should survive the attack. Alekhine must keep as many pieces on the board as he can.

30 Re1 Qd8
However, this move, offering a queen exchange, is too passive. Grunfeld should have tried more active play, such as 30 ...Qxd4 or 30 ...Rc3, when Alekhine would still have to work hard to keep the attack going.

31 Qh6 Qf8?
The same mistake as on the previous move. He should have gone for 31 ...Qxd4. As played, he gives Alekhine a new attacking plan.

32 Kg2!
With the idea of 33 Rh1 and 34 Qh8 checkmate. The black queen has rather clumsily denied her king a flight square.

32 ... Ne8
33 Qh4 Qxa3
34 Rh1 Kf8
35 Qg5!

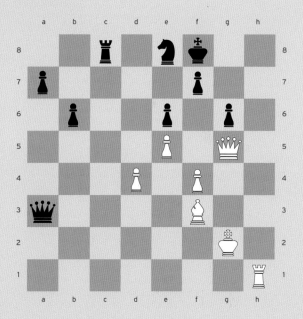

Black's king cannot evacuate the kingside. The immediate threat is 36 Rh8+ Kg7 37 Qh6 checkmate and there is no effective defence. 36 ...Kg8, to defend h8, runs into 37 Qh6 and checkmate follows. Black resigned. **1-0**

CLASSIC PLAYERS AND GAMES

It is an impossible task to decide who is the greatest of all chess players. We can play through games going back hundreds of years, we can compare the results of thousands of matches and tournaments and we can look at their respective ratings, but we can never see all of the finest players who ever lived competing against each other.

We can, however, compile a list of all those players who won the world title and make some informed judgements.

The first official World Championship match was won by Wilhelm Steinitz. He defeated Johannes Zukertort in 1886. Before that, a number of players had a perfect right to think of themselves as the best in the world, including André Philidor, Louis Charles de la Bourdonnais, Howard Staunton, Adolf Anderssen and Paul Morphy, but then there was no official match for the title.

For a long time, after 1886, the champion was more or less able to decide who his next challenger should be. This was a far from perfect system and it changed for the better when FIDE (the world organisational body for chess) took control of the championship in 1948, and imposed a three year cycle of qualification tournaments and matches to decide the next world title challenger.

But, in 1993, came a big split in world chess. World Champion Garry Kasparov and his challenger, Nigel Short, opted out of the FIDE system and played their match under the auspices of the Professional Chess Association ('PCA'). FIDE quickly arranged their own title match and for a while there were two world champions. This unsatisfactory state of affairs was finally resolved in 2007 and we currently have an undisputed world champion once again.

Official Matches for the World Championship, 1886-1937:

1886: Wilhelm Steinitz beats Johannes Zukertort (+10, -5, =5)

1889: Wilhelm Steinitz beats Mikhail Chigorin (+10, -6, =1)

1890-1: Wilhelm Steinitz beats Isidor Gunsberg (+6, -4, =9)

1892: Wilhelm Steinitz beats Mikhail Chigorin (+10, -8, =5)

1894: Emanuel Lasker beats Wilhelm Steinitz (+10, -5, =4)

1897: Emanuel Lasker beats Wilhelm Steinitz (+10, -2, =5)

1907: Emanuel Lasker beats Frank James Marshall (+8, -0, =7)

1908: Emanuel Lasker beats Siegbert Tarrasch (+8, -3, =5)

1910: Emanuel Lasker draws with Karl Schlechter (+1, -1, =8)

1910: Emanuel Lasker beats Janowsky (+8, -0, =3)

1921: José Raul Capablanca beats Emanuel Lasker (+4, -0, =10)

1927: Alexander Alekhine beats José Raul Capablanca (+6, -3, =25)

1929: Alexander Alekhine beats Efim Bogoljubov (+11, -5, =9)

1934: Alexander Alekhine beats Efim Bogoljubov (+8, -3, =15)

1935: Max Euwe beats Alexander Alekhine (+9, -8, =13)

1937: Alexander Alekhine beats Max Euwe (+10, -4, =11)

Alexander Alekhine died in 1946, the only occasion to date that a World Champion has taken the title to the grave. FIDE then took control of the World Championship and organised a tournament featuring most of the top players of the time.

1948: World Championship tournament won by Mikhail Botvinnik

After this, FIDE introduced a regular three year cycle of Zonal, Interzonal and Candidates qualifiers to decide the next world title challenger. This provided stability for the next 45 years. The qualification system in place was geared towards producing a world title challenger every three years. Matches were scheduled to last for 24 games and a 12-12 result would see the champion retain his title. The champion was given the right to a return match if he lost his title. During this period, Russian players dominated, with the sole exception of the American, Bobby Fischer.

1951: Mikhail Botvinnik draws with David Bronstein (+5, -5, =14)

1954: Mikhail Botvinnik draws with Vassily Smyslov (+7, -7, =10)

1957: Vassily Smyslov beats Mikhail Botvinnik (+6, -3, =13)

1958: Mikhail Botvinnik beats Vassily Smyslov (+7, -5, =11)

1960: Mikhail Tal beats Mikhail Botvinnik (+6, -2, =13)

1961: Mikhail Botvinnik beats Mikhail Tal (+10, -5, =6)

1963: Tigran Petrosian beats Mikhail Botvinnk (+5, -2, =15)

At this point, FIDE abolished the right for a return match and Botvinnik retired from his battles for the World Championship.

1966: Tigran Petrosian beats Boris Spassky (+4, -3, =17)

1969: Boris Spassky beats Tigran Petrosian (+6, -4, =13)

1972: Bobby Fischer beats Boris Spassky (+7, -3, =11)

1975: Anatoly Karpov wins the title by default.

Bobby Fischer, in dispute with FIDE over the match conditions, declined to play his official challenger. He didn't play another competitive game for 20 years. FIDE then changed the match rules from a set 24 games to an open-ended match requiring six wins for victory, with draws not counting.

1978: Anatoly Karpov beats Viktor Korchnoi (+6, -5, =21)

1981: Anatoly Karpov beats Viktor Korchnoi (+6, -2 =10)

1984: Anatoly Karpov vs. Garry Kasparov – match aborted (+5, -3 =40)

The first Karpov vs. Kasparov match ended in controversy when FIDE terminated it, with Karpov 5-3 ahead. He had been leading 5-0 at one point but Kasparov fought back towards the end of the match. After 48 games – exactly twice as long as one of the traditional, 24 gamematches – it was brought to an end, a decision which left both players feeling very frustrated and angry. A rematch was announced for the following year, but it was to be played under the old 24 game rules – with draws counting again.

1985: Garry Kasparov beats Anatoly Karpov (+5, -3, =16)

1986: Garry Kasparov beats Anatoly Karpov (+5, -4, =15)

1987: Garry Kasparov draws with Anatoly Karpov (+4, -4, =16)

1990: Garry Kasparov beats Anatoly Karpov (+4, -3, =17)

Then came the above-mentioned shock split. Garry Kasparov and his challenger, Nigel Short, broke away from FIDE to play their 1993 match under the auspices of the newly-formed Professional Chess Association ('PCA'). Upon this FIDE quickly arranged a match of their own between Anatoly Karpov and Jan

Timman (each of whom had lost Candidates matches against Short).

PCA Titles

1993:   Garry Kasparov beats Nigel Short (+6, -1, =13)

1995:   Garry Kasparov beats Viswanathan Anand (+4, -1, =13)

To add to the confusion, the PCA folded soon after the Anand match. Negotiations came and went for other potential matches but it wasn't until five years later that Kasparov played again for the title.

Classical World Chess Championship

2000:   Vladimir Kramnik beats Garry Kasparov (+2, -0, =13)

FIDE Titles

1993:   Anatoly Karpov beats Jan Timman (+6, -2, =13)

1996:   Anatoly Karpov beats Gata Kamsky (+6, -3, =9)

FIDE changed the rules again for the 1998 contest. They decided on an annual knock-out tournament instead of traditional matches.

FIDE KO World Champions

1998:   Anatoly Karpov

1999:   Alexander Khalifman

2000: Viswanathan Anand

2001:   Ruslan Ponomariov

2004:   Rustam Kasimdzhanov

Various attempts were made to unite the two titles, but these were unsuccessful for a number of years.

Classical World Chess Championship

2004:   Vladimir Kramnik draws with Peter Leko (+2, -2, =10)

In 2005, Garry Kasparov announced his retirement from competitive chess and FIDE announced a new World Championship tournament. Kramnik declined to play.

FIDE World Championship Tournament

2005:   Winner – Veselin Topalov

Negotiations now took place to arrange a match between the two champions, Kramnik and Topalov, under the auspices of FIDE. It was a very controversial match but it finally united the two branches of the World Championship.

FIDE World Championship Match

2006: Vladimir Kramnik beats Veselin Topalov (+5, -4, =7)

FIDE organized another World Championship tournament for the following year. Kramnik, the undisputed World Champion, agreed to participate but he did not win the tournament.

FIDE World Championship Tournament

2007:   Winner – Viswanathan Anand

Then it was back to traditional matches, albeit with just 12 games instead of 24.

FIDE World Champions

2008: Viswanathan Anand beats Vladimir Kramnik (+3, -1, =7)

2010: Viswanathan Anand beats Veselin Topalov (+3, -2, =7)

2012: Viswanathan Anand beats Boris Gelfand (+2, -1, =13)

2013: Magnus Carlsen beats Viswanathan Anand (+3, -0, = 7)

Magnus Carlsen, from Norway, became the second-youngest World Champion in history at the age of 22 years and eleven months (behind Garry Kasparov's 22 years and six months, when he won the title in 1985).

2014: Magnus Carlsen beats Viswanathan Anand (+3, -1, =7)

2016: Magnus Carlsen beats Sergey Karjakin (+1, -1, =10; Carlsen wins the tie-breaker Rapid games, 3-1)

2018: Magnus Carlsen beats Fabiano Caruana (+0, -0, =10; Carlsen wins the tie-breaker Rapid games, 3-0)

Instructive Games by World Chess Champions

It would be a mistake to think the best games of the old champions are in any way less instructive than those of today. We have already examined some games by Tal, Petrosian, Fischer, Karpov and Kasparov in the chapter, Know Your Openings (pages 126-83). Now we present a small selection of games which show other champions in action.

In 1834, the Frenchman Louis-Charles de la Bourdonnais played a series of matches against the Irishman Alexander McDonnell in a kind of unofficial match for the World Championship. They played 85 games in all, with the final score of +45, -27, =13 in de la Bourdonnais's favour. The games of their matches are fascinating, even to modern eyes. They show chess evolution in action, with both players adapting their chess openings and styles throughout the match and having to constantly devise new ideas to outwit each other. They played a wide variety of openings, including the Queen's Gambit, the King's Gambit and the Sicilian Defence.

1 e4 e5
2 f4 exf4
The King's Gambit Accepted.

3 Nf3 g5
4 Bc4 g4
5 Nc3
This branch of the King's Gambit is still known as the McDonnell Gambit. (It does not currently enjoy a good reputation.) McDonnell is fully prepared to sacrifice his king's knight as long as he can achieve the rapid development of his other pieces. The logic behind the idea is that de la Bourdonnais will now have to spend even more time on pawn moves – and will have to defend carefully while he tries to catch up with his opponent in piece development.

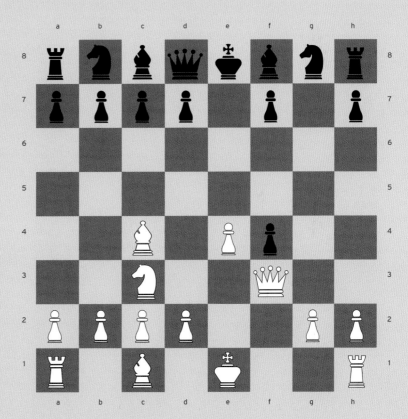

Alexander McDonnell vs. Louis-Charles de la Bourdonnais
Game 54, London, 1834

position after 6 Qxf3

5 ...gxf3
6 Qxf3

McDonnell is a knight down. Does the extra space, better pawn structure and big lead in development provide enough compensation?

6 ...Bh6

De la Bourdonnais plays to defend his f4-pawn for as long as possible, in an attempt to keep potential lines of attack against his king closed.

7 d4 Nc6
8 0-0!
8 ...Nxd4

Continuing his policy of development over material.

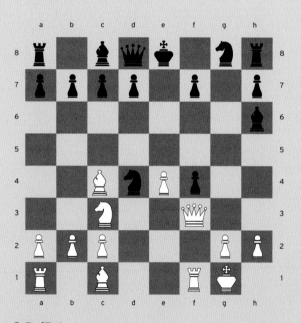

9 Bxf7+!

This is a frequently seen move in the King's Gambit, which strips away an important defensive pawn and drags the opponent's king out of his lair.

9 ...Kxf7
10 Qh5+ Kg7
11 Bxf4 Bxf4

12 Rxf4 Nf6
13 Qg5+ Kf7
14 Raf1

McDonnell has built up a winning attack almost effortlessly, in the style of the great Greco. De la Bourdonnais must lose his king's knight due to the pin and his king will not be able to find anywhere to hide.

14 ...Ke8
15 Rxf6 Qe7

Looking for counterplay with his queen and at the same time freeing a potential flight square on d8 for the king.

16 Nd5!

More fuel on the fire!

16 ...Qc5

One last try. If McDonnell loses concentration he could miss the discovered check with 17 ...Nf3+! followed by 18 ...Nxg5, when suddenly he has a lost position.

17 Kh1! Ne6

McDonnell finishes off with another sacrifice.

**18 Rxe6+! dxe6
19 Nf6+**

Thanks to this deadly discovered attack, McDonnell will capture the queen on the next move, no matter how la Bourdonnais escapes from check. De la Bourdonnais resigned here. **1-0**

Alexander McDonnell vs. Louis-Charles de la Bourdonnais

Game 62, London, 1834

1 e4 c5

It is interesting to note that de la Bourdonnais switched to the Sicilian Defence following his unpleasant experiences against the King's Gambit.

**2 Nf3 Nc6
3 d4 cxd4
4 Nxd4 e5**

White's best move now is 5 Nb5, hoping to invade on the d6 square. With the move played in the game, McDonnell merely allows de la Bourdonnais to strengthen his pawn centre. It should be kept in mind that the players were entering brand new territory at the time and there was little or no theory on what we now class as main lines of the Sicilian Defence.

**5 Nxc6 bxc6
6 Bc4**

McDonnell will have an advantage if he can prevent de la Bourdonnais from playing ...d7-d5, establishing a very strong pawn centre. This and the next few moves are all about the struggle for the d5 square.

6 ...Nf6

Threatening 7 ...d5 again. 6 ...d5 here would have been a blunder due to 7 exd5 cxd5 8 B(orQ)xd5.

7 Bg5

The pin on the knight makes 7 ...d5 undesirable again.

7 ...Be7

Breaking the pin and renewing the threat.

8 Qe2

8 Nc3, keeping alive the struggle for d5, would have been more consistent. De la Bourdonnais is now able to achieve his aim. 8 Qe2 appears to have been played in the hope of applying indirect pressure on the e-pawn, but after 8 ...d5! 9 cxd5 cxd5 McDonnell would be unable to play 10 Qxe5 because of 10 ...dxc4.

8 ...d5	**11 0-0 a5**
9 Bxf6 Bxf6	**12 exd5 cxd5**
10 Bb3 0-0	

13 Rd1 d4
14 c4 Qb6
15 Bc2 Bb7
16 Nd2 Rae8
17 Ne4 Bd8
18 c5 Qc6
19 f3 Be7
20 Rac1

McDonnell has done well to inject some life into his position. He appears to have his opponent's central pawns blockaded, while his passed c-pawn is surviving thanks to a tactical motif: 20 ...Bxc5?? 21 Nxc5 Qxc5?? would lose the queen to a discovered attack - 22 Bxh7+! Kxh7 23 Rxc5. However, with his next move, de la Bourdonnais re-energizes his centre and produces a massive pawn roller that will make a decisive impact on the course of the game.

20 ...f5!

This may look simple enough to modern eyes but de la Bourdonnais had to take into account McDonnell's next three moves - during which the latter wins the exchange (a rook for a bishop) - and to assess whether or not the material imbalance was relevant.

21 Qc4+ Kh8
22 Ba4

A skewer, made possible by the queen's protection of the a4 square with gain of tempo.

22 ...Qh6
23 Bxe8 fxe4
24 c6 exf3

The pawns acquire new strength. Now McDonnell cannot capture the bishop, as after the tempting 25 cxb7?? comes 25 ...Qe3+ and the direct attack on the king will prove fatal.

25 Rc2!

Protecting the important f2 and g2 squares. Defending laterally along a rank, with queens and rooks, is a technique worth remembering.

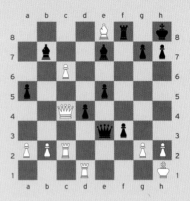

25 ...Qe3+
26 Kh1

A very complicated position.

26 ...Bc8

26 ...Ba8 (to keep the bishop on the same line as McDonnell's king) and 26 ....d3 were other options worthy of consideration. After the latter, a sample line goes: 26 Qxd3 (26 Rxd3?? Qe1 checkmate) 26 ...Qxd3 27 Rxd3 f2! (threatening to promote the pawn with 28 ...f1=Q checkmate) 28 Rxf2 Rxf2 (threatening checkmate yet again, this time with 28 ...Rf1) 29 Kg1 Bc5! with threats of various deadly discovered checks following a move of the f2 rook.

27 Bd7 f2
28 Rf1 d3
29 Rc3 Bxd7
30 cxd7 e4

The thoughts of both players will be dominated by two concerns: how to stop the opponent's passed pawn(s) and how to promote their own.

31 Qc8

A standard tactical device, offering the queen for greater gain. Now 31 ...Rxc8?? 32 dxc8=Q+ and checkmate on the next move is out of the question. There is a threat too: 32 Qxf8+ Bxf8 33 d8=Q, with a winning advantage for McDonnell. De la Bourdonnais rushes to halt the advance of the highly dangerous c-pawn.

31 ...Bd8
32 Qc4

Giving up his aggressive intentions and dashing back to try to stop the menacing army of pawns. Unfortunately, they prove to be too strong and the game heads for a beautiful finale.

32 ...Qe1!
33 Rc1 d2
34 Qc5 Rg8!

There was still a chance to go wrong. An excited player can lose focus and McDonnell was threatening 35 Qxf8 checkmate! De la Bourdonnais spotted the threat and made a defensive move before continuing his attack.

35 Rd1 e3
36 Qc3 Qxd1
37 Rxd1 e2

An extraordinary position, fully demonstrating the power of passed pawns. McDonnell has no way of meeting all of the threats, so he resigned, **0-1**

Paul Morphy was a chess player ahead of his time. But he gave up chess prematurely, having crushed all of his opponents. His games were always instructive and well worth playing through.

In 1858 Morphy contested a match with Adolf Anderssen and won with the score of seven wins, two draws and two losses. Anderssen had previously won the world's first international tournament, in 1851, and dazzled the world with his exceptional tactical flair. His match with Morphy can be seen as a pivotal point in the history of chess. Morphy's modern style of play proved to be too tough a nut for the leader of the old guard to crack. It was no longer enough to play a sharp and possibly reckless gambit in order to gain an attack. Anderssen's preferred method of play simply left too many weaknesses which Morphy was able to exploit.

Paul Morphy vs. Adolf Anderssen
Paris, 1858

1 e4 c5

In an age of King's Gambits and Evans Gambits, the Sicilian was still comparatively rare in games between top players. This was the first – and last – time Anderssen played this defence against Morphy and he suffers a catastrophic defeat. Nowadays, of course, it is one of the most popular of all openings

2 Nf3 Nc6
3 d4 cxd4
4 Nxd4 e6
5 Nb5 d6
6 Bf4 e5
7 Be3 f5

A risky move. Anderssen had already tried 7 ...a6 in a game against Szen at the London tournament. He lost that game and 7 ...f5 is his intended improvement. Morphy meets this extravagant pawn thrust with classical development.

8 N1c3 f4

8 ...a6 was the best try, but Morphy could still continue with 9 Nd5 axb5 10 Bb6 and fork with 11 Nc7+

9 Nd5 fxe3

It was already too late for Black to change his mind. He had to capture the bishop and allow the forthcoming knight fork. Perhaps he thought he could trap the knight in the corner but it all looks like an experiment gone badly wrong.

10 Nbc7+ Kf7

There's nothing wrong with simply taking the rook by 11 Nxa8. Black's counterattack soon runs

out of steam after 11 ...exf2+ 12 Kxf2 Qh4+ 13 g3 Qxe4 14 Bg2 Qf5+ 15 Kg1. Morphy decides to keep his king as safe as possible, whilst continuing his own attack.

11 Qf3+ Nf6
12 Bc4

Developing another piece and setting up a dangerous discovered check.

12 ...Nd4

Anderssen continues to neglect his defence and insists on pursuing his own attack.

13 Nxf6+ d5
14 Bxd5+ Kg6

A mistake, played under tremendous pressure. It's always very difficult to pick one's way through a minefield when the king is exposed. Anderssen still had two (very complicated) ways to try to survive, namely 14 ...Ke7 and 14 ...Qxd5. After 14 ...Kg6 his position is completely lost.

15 Qh5+ Kxf6
16 fxe3 Nxc2+
17 Ke2

Black's big problem is that his king will be checked by the white rook. If, for example, he plays 17 ...Nxa1 there comes a forced checkmate with 18 Rf1+ Ke7 19 Qxe5+ Kd7 20 Be6+ Kc6 21 Rc1+ Nc2 22 Rxc2+ Kb6 23 Qb5 mate. **1-0**

Alexander Alekhine was as obsessed by chess as anyone. He played and analysed constantly, always looking to deepen his understanding of the game. He was capable of whipping up a devastating attack at almost any time.

He only ever beat Emanuel Lasker once, but it was with one of his trademark mating attacks.

Alexander Alekhine vs. Emanuel Lasker
Zurich, 1934

1 d4 d5
2 c4 e6
3 Nc3 Nf6
4 Nf3 Be7
5 Bg5 Nbd7
6 e3 0-0

Lasker has defended very solidly against the Queen's Gambit. Over the course of the next few moves he aims to simplify the position with exchanges.

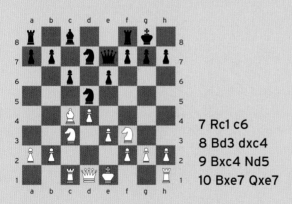

7 Rc1 c6
8 Bd3 dxc4
9 Bxc4 Nd5
10 Bxe7 Qxe7

Alekhine, who always preferred complicated positions, strives to keep as many pieces on the board as possible.

11 Ne4 N5f6
12 Ng3 e5

Black can feel happy with the way the opening has gone. The liberating break 12 ...e5 usually achieves equality. Note that the queen's bishop will soon be able to enter the game.

13 0-0 exd4
13 ...e4, pushing away the white knight and gaining space in the centre, should have been preferred. Lasker sticks to his policy of keeping things as simple as possible, but Alekhine now injects more life into the position.

14 Nf5 Qd8
15 N3xd4 Ne5
16 Bb3 Bxf5
17 Nxf5 Qb6
18 Qd6 Ned7
19 Rfd1 Rad8

Alekhine had a terrific knack of getting the most out of his pieces. Lasker's position still looks solid enough – after all, he has made no obvious mistakes – but after the next move he suddenly finds his king facing a direct attack.

20 Qg3 g6
The last thing Black wanted was to create a serious weakness in his defensive pawn structure, but he was remarkably short of options. 20 ...Ne8 fails to 21 Nh6+ (exploiting the pin on the g-pawn) 21 ...Kh8 22 Nxf7+ with a winning attack. 20 ... Nh5 defends against the threat of checkmate on g7 and attacks the queen, but after 21 Qg5, he will have to play 21 ...g6 anyway and this time it's even worse than in the game, as his knight is badly misplaced on h5.

21 Qg5 Kh8
22 Nd6 Kg7
23 e4

Another powerful move. Alekhine introduces two new threats: e4-e5, to chase away the knight, and a rook lift to the third rank, where it can swing across to assist the queen in attacking the black king.

23 ...Ng8
24 Rd3 f6

Lasker cracks under the pressure. His position is clearly very difficult, but this further weakening of his pawn shield leads to a forced checkmate.

25 Nf5+ Kh8
26 Qxg6

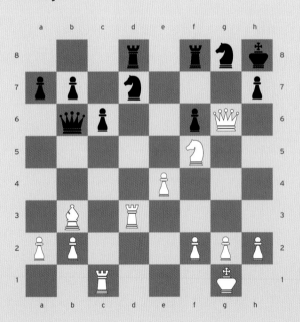

Absolutely typical of Alekhine. Now 26 ...hxg6 allows a checkmate after 27 Rh3+ Nh6 28 Rxh6 checkmate (note the bishop on b3, stopping the black king from running to g8). Meanwhile, there is no way to prevent a checkmate on g7 by the white queen. Black resigned. **1-0**

Botvinnik and Smyslov fought three matches for the World Championship (1954, 1957 and 1958). Only the rivalry between Karpov and Kasparov - who contested five matches against each other (1984, 1985, 1986, 1987 and 1990) - can match that. Indeed, Botvinnik and Smyslov met many times over the chess board, away from title matches too. They first played each other in 1941 and faced each other for the last time in 1969.

Mikhail Botvinnik vs. Vassily Smyslov
USSR Championship, Moscow, 1945

1 d4 d5
2 Nf3 Nf6
3 c4 c6

The Slav Defence to the Queen's Gambit was Smyslov's favourite throughout his lengthy career. Botvinnik's next move - introducing the Exchange Variation - is not reckoned to be the most challenging of White's options, but it can lead to a slight advantage.

4 cxd5 cxd5
5 Nc3 Nc6
6 Bf4 e6
7 e3 Be7
8 Bd3 0-0
9 h3 Bd7
10 0-0 a6

The players have reached a solid position. However, Black's queen's bishop is somewhat lacking in scope and he therefore suffers from a very slight disadvantage.

11 Rc1 Be8
12 Bb1 Nh5
13 Bh2 f5

This is ambitious play by Smyslov. By adopting a Stonewall formation, he is preparing to attack on the kingside by means of ...g5 and ...g4. He has also increased the scope of his queen's bishop, but left a couple of weaknesses on the queenside which Botvinnik quickly tries to exploit.

14 Na4 Bd6	**16 Nxh2 Qe7**
15 Nc5 Bxh2+	**17 Qb3 Rf7**

Botvinink's next move is a surprise. It is normally inadvisable to meet pawn storms with pawn moves, as this makes it easier for the opponent to open attacking lines. Yet Botvinnik's deep idea is to create pressure on both the kingside and the queenside.

18 g4 fxg4
19 hxg4 Nf6
20 f4

Here, Smyslov should probably take a leaf out of Botvinnik's book and reroute his queen's knight with 20 ...Na5 and 21 ...Nc4. Instead he chooses to sacrifice his queenside pawns in order to lure the white queen away from her protection of the other side of the board. After this he hopes to launch a direct attack on the white king.

20 ...b6
21 Qxb6 Rb8
22 Qxa6 e5

Smyslov is obliged to sacrifice more material to justify his previous play.

23 dxe5 Nxe5	**25 Qe6 Qg3+**
24 fxe5 Qxe5	**26 Kh1 Rxb2**

This is as good as it's going to get for Black. He threatens checkmate by his queen on both g2 and h2, but Botvinnik has everything under control and now forces away the two main attackers.

27 Rc2 Rb8
28 Rg2 Qh4
29 g5 Nh5
30 g6 hxg6
31 Bxg6

The pin on the rook (by White's queen) prevents 31 ...Rxf1+. Moreover, 32 Bxf7+ is coming next, increasing White's already considerable material advantage. Smyslov saw no good way of continuing the game and resigned. **1-0**

Boris Spassky's style of play has often been described as 'universal' – meaning he could attack as brilliantly as he could defend. He could also play virtually any opening equally well. His greatest strength was in the middlegame. A 'universal' approach enables a player to adapt his play to the particular features of an opponent's style and focus on weak aspects of his game. Against the brilliant tactician, Mikhail Tal, it was advisable to keep the position as quiet as possible. Attacking players can lose their patience in such positions and make premature attempts to create tactical opportunities.

Boris Spassky vs. Mikhail Tal
USSR Championship, Baku, 1961

1 d4 Nf6
2 Nf3

Already a shrewd choice. Tal had swept away all opposition on his way to becoming World Champion in 1960 by playing openings such as the Modern Benoni (1 d4 Nf6 2 c4 c5 3 d5 e6). With 2 Nf3, Spassky shows that he is not going to enter the main line Benoni, thus steering Tal

away from his favourite playing field.

2 ...g6

Tal was equally at home in wild King's Indian positions. Spassky again keeps things as quiet as possible and refuses to go down a main line.

3 g3 Bg7
4 Bg2 c5
5 c4 0-0
6 0-0 d6
7 Nc3 Nc6

Normally White would continue with 8 d5 here, consolidating his big centre and space advantage. But then Black would have a definite target to attack. Spassky plays a move, long considered harmless but all part of his game plan.

8 dxc5 dxc5

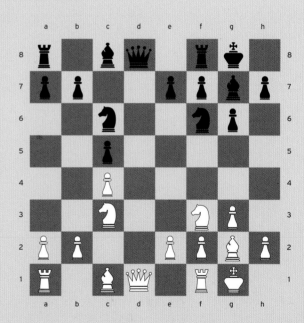

Most Grandmasters would find such a symmetrical position easy to draw. It's hard to imagine either side achieving a decisive advantage from here.

9 Be3 Be6
10 Bxc5 Qa5
11 Ba3 Bxc4
12 Nd4 Nxd4
13 Qxd4 Rac8

Tal is trying to complicate the position. He is allowing a choice of two captures: 14 Bxb7 and 14 Bxe7. He plans to meet either capture with the tricky 14 ...Nd5, attacking the white queen and activating his king's bishop.

14 Qf4 g5

This loosening move shows that Tal is losing patience and trying to force the issue. However he only succeeds in weakening his position. 14 ...Nh5 would be a better choice when, after 15 Qf3, he could defend both pawns with 15 ...Rc7. 14 ...Rc7, without the preliminary knight move, doesn't work because of 14 Bxe7 Rxe7 15 Qxc4 and White is a sound pawn up.

15 Qe3 Rc7
16 Rad1 Re8
17 Rd4 b5

This is a big mistake. Spassky is now able to exploit the undefended g5-pawn. Tal is hoping for tricks with an eventual ...b4, potentially forking two of White's pieces, but he should have defended g5 with 17 ...h6 before embarking on such tactical adventures.

18 Qxg5 h6

Not 18 ...b4 here, because the b-pawn is pinned by the white queen (19 Qxa5).

19 Qd2 b4
20 Nb1

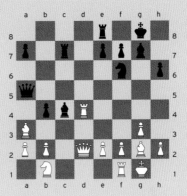

Once again the b-pawn is pinned by the white queen.

20 ...Nd5
21 Rg4 h5
22 Rg5

A plethora of pins. The white rook pins the bishop and knight and the queen continues to pin the b-pawn. It seems that every time Tal tries to generate some activity, he is immediately held back. There follows a flurry of tactical moves, but Spassky retains complete control and ends up with an easily winning endgame.

22 ...Rc5
23 b3 Nc3
24 Rxc5 Qxc5
25 Nxc3 bxc3
26 Bxc5 cxd2
27 bxc4 Rb8
28 Bxa7 Rb2
29 e3 Rxa2

Black is a piece and a pawn down. He might as well resign here but plays on for a little while longer to see if he can make anything of his passed d-pawn. Unfortunately for him, he will never be able to take control of the all-important queening square on d1 – simply because White has more pieces operating on the white squares.

30 Bc5 e5
31 Bf3 h4
32 Rd1 hxg3
33 hxg3 Rc2
34 Be2 Rb2
35 Bd3

Tal now resigned. **1-0**

A very good example of how to deal with highly dangerous tactical players. Incidentally, Spassky went on to win the USSR Championship that year, half a point ahead of Lev Polugaevsky.

Veselin Topalov united the two branches of the World Chess Championship when he won a strong world title tournament at San Luis, Argentina, in 2007. His aggressive style of play and excellent tactical ability gave him a chance of winning against anyone. Back in 1994, he was already capable of beating the best, as he demonstrated in the following game against the reigning champion.

Veselin Topalov vs. Garry Kasparov
Chess Olympiad, Moscow 1994

1 e4 c5
2 Nf3 d6
3 d4 cxd4
4 Nxd4 Nf6
5 Nc3 a6

As we saw in the chapter on openings, Kasparov consistently played the Sicilian Defence and the Najdorf variation in particular. Topalov opts for a very aggressive response.

6 Be3 e6
7 g4 h6
8 f4 Nc6
9 Be2 e5

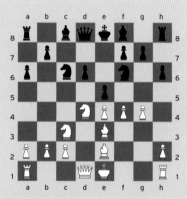

A standard central thrust, often effective when the opponent advances pawns on the flank.

10 Nf5 g6
11 Ng3 exf4
12 Bxf4 Be6
13 Rf1 Rc8
14 h3 Qb6

14 ...d5 looks like Black's best move. Kasparov wants to obtain more from the position but has to take risks to do so.

15 Qd2 Bg7

If Black could safely castle his king with ...0-0, he would stand well, but he has weak pawns on d6 and h6. It was rare indeed for Kasparov to leave his king in the centre and here he pays for his neglect of king safety.

16 Bxd6 Nxg4

19 Rb1 Qxc3
20 Qxc3 Rxc3
21 Bxe6 fxe6
22 Rxb7 Nc4
23 Bb4 Re3+
24 Ne2 Be5
25 Rff7 Rxh3

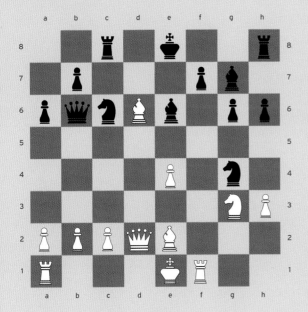

Both kings are under fire but White has more attacking units. If Topalov could shift the black bishop from e5, he could force a quick checkmate with Rfe7 followed by Rb8. His next move offers a knight as bait but, as Black can't afford to take it, this piece is then able to enter the attack with decisive effect.

26 Nd4 Re3+
27 Kf1 Re4
28 Rfe7+ Kd8
29 Nc6+

A typically dynamic idea from Kasparov. By sacrificing a knight, he has opened up his king's bishop. He hopes the bishop will have a decisive influence along the long diagonal once he has softened it up with ...Qxb2. Yet Topalov is more than equal to the tactical task.

17 Bxg4 Qxb2
18 e5 Nxe5

The tempting 18 ...Qxa1+ leaves Black's queen in too much trouble after 19 Kf2 (19 ...Qb2 20 Rb1). There now follows a tactical sequence which turns out better for White, as he establishes both of his rooks on the seventh rank.

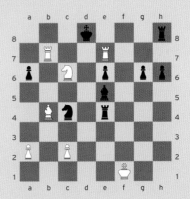

This is just the sort of thing Kasparov dealt out to others on a very regular basis. It's checkmate in two more moves: 29 ...Kc8 30 Na7+ Kd8 31 Rad7, so he resigned.

1-0

Vladimir Kramnik and Viswanathan Anand have enjoyed a long chess rivalry but have remained good friends. They played a title match in 2008 and Anand emerged victorious, thanks mainly to his fine play with the black pieces.

Vladimir Kramnik vs. Viswanathan Anand

Game 5, World Championship Match, Bonn, 2008

1 d4 d5
2 c4 c6
3 Nf3 Nf6
4 Nc3 e6

Combining the Orthodox move ...e6 with the Slav's ...c6 forms the Semi-Slav Defence. It has served Anand well and was also a favourite of Botvinnik. Play can become very sharp early on in the game.

5 e3 Nbd7	**9 e4 c5**	**13 0-0 Qb6**
6 Bd3 dxc4	**10 e5 cxd4**	**14 Qe2 Bb7**
7 Bxc4 b5	**11 Nxb5 axb5**	**15 Bxb5 Rg8**
8 Bd3 a6	**12 exf6 gxf6**	

All theory! Modern chess Grandmasters have to store a lot of information in their heads. One cannot hope to survive in long theoretical lines without memorizing - and, more importantly, understanding - long sequences of moves. Anand played 15 ...Bd6 in the third game of the match and won. This time he plays something different.

16 Bf4 Bd6
17 Bg3 f5
18 Rfc1 f4
19 Bh4 Be7

This is a complicated position and very difficult to handle from either side of the board. White's king should be safer than Black's because he has castled, but the rook on g8 represents a serious danger. Meanwhile, White has a pair of connected passed pawns on the queenside and he may think the black king - stuck in the middle - is an easier target than his own.

20 a4 Bxh4	**25 Qg4 Qe5**
21 Nxh4 Ke7	**26 Nf3 Qf6**
22 Ra3 Rac8	**27 Re1 Rc5**
23 Rxc8 Rxc8	**28 b4**
24 Ra1 Qc5	

Black can now initiate a trade of knights with 28 ...Ne5, but he prefers something more ambitious.

28 ...Rc3
29 Nxd4 Qxd4
30 Rd1

This pin looks fatal, since a queen move would allow 31 Rxd7+ with an easy win. However, Anand has a surprising resource...

30 ...Nf6

...and suddenly White is struggling to hold everything together.

31 Rxd4 Nxg4
32 Rd7+ Kf6
33 Rxb7 Rc1+
34 Bf1

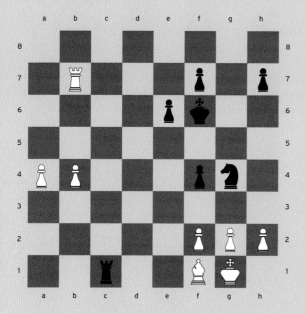

At first glance White appears to be fine here. His passed pawns look like winners, but it turns out that Anand has seen a little further and he concludes the game with a deft stroke.

34 ...Ne3
35 fxe3 fxe3

There is no sensible way of preventing the winning move 36 ...e2 (winning the bishop and gaining a new queen) so Kramnik had to resign.

0-1

Viswanathan Anand vs. Magnus Carlsen

Game 9, World Championship Match, Chennai, 2013

After eight games of the 2013 World Championship match, the champion was trailing by two points. He needed two wins from the last four games to force the match into extra time. Game 9 was his last big push with the white pieces.

1 d4

Anand had failed to gain an advantage with 1 e4, earlier in the match, so here he switches openings to test the other side of Carlsen's repertoire.

1 ...Nf6
2 c4 e6
3 Nc3 Bb4

The Nimzo-Indian Defence remains a powerful weapon in Black's armoury. It is no surprise to see Carlsen using it in this key game.

4 f3 d5
5 a3 Bxc3+
6 bxc3 c5
7 cxd5 exd5
8 e3 c4
9 Ne2 Nc6
10 g4

Anand signals his aggressive intentions. This move is very much in the style of Botvinnik and Kasparov, each of whom enjoyed a great deal of success from similar positions.

10 ...0-0
11 Bg2 Na5
12 0-0 Nb3

White will continue to push for an attack on the kingside and Black will take pleasure in raiding White's weakened queenside. The game is unlikely to end in a draw as it is so unbalanced.

13 Ra2 b5
14 Ng3 a5
15 g5 Ne8
16 e4 Nxc1
17 Qxc1 Ra6

18 e5 Nc7
19 f4 b4
20 axb4 axb4
21 Rxa6 Nxa6
22 f5 b3

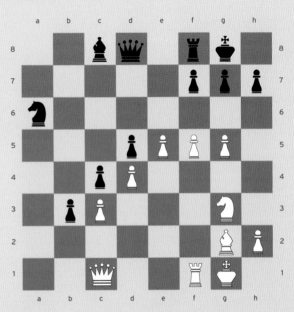

If Anand's kingside attack falters, then Carlsen's passed b-pawn - so close to promotion - will decide the game.

23 Qf4 Nc7
24 f6 g6

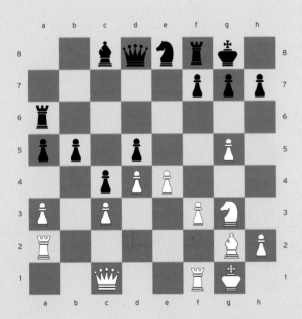

Both rooks on the queenside are able to influence the action on the other wing by sweeping across their respective second ranks.

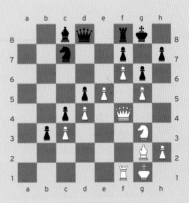

White's attack looks very dangerous. Black's knight is just able to hold things together by defending g7.

**25 Qh4 Ne8
26 Qh6 b2
27 Rf4 b1=Q+**

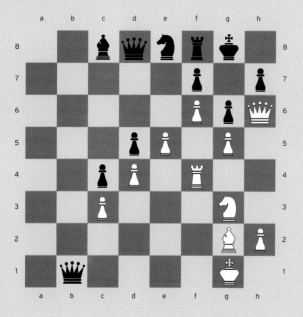

A fabulous position! Anand has allowed Carlsen to obtain a second queen. If the champion doesn't find the correct continuation for his kingside attack then the material disadvantage will prove fatal.

28 Nf1??
A big mistake. He had to play 28 Bf1! when one possible line goes: 28 ...Qd1 29 Rh4 Qh5! (giving up his extra queen to prevent checkmate) 30 Nxh5 gxh5 31 Rxh5 Bf5 (defending the key h7 square) 32 g6! Bxg5 33 Rxg5 when the position is very unclear. After the move played, Anand has a lost position.

28 ...Qe1!

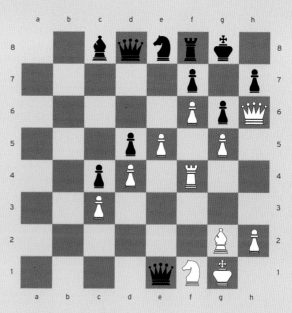

A simple enough move for Carlsen to find. 29 Rh4 Qxh4 would end the attack for good and leave Black with a great material advantage. Seeing no other way to continue the game, Anand resigned, **0-1**.

This magnificent battle from the 2013 World Chess Championship brings our current chess journey to an end. I sincerely hope you have enjoyed reading this book and I wish you good fortune in your future chess battles.

Solutions

Solutions to Puzzles from British Championship 2013

Gawain Jones vs. John Reid: 33 Rxc5+ bxc5 34 Qb2, forking the rook on h8 and the b8 square (planning 35 Qb8 checkmate). 1-0

Mark Hebden vs. Colin Purdon: 50 Ba6+! A discovered attack, winning the queen. 1-0

Alan Brusey vs. Charles Storey: 37 ...Rxg3 38 Rxg3 Rxg3 39 Qxg3 Qe2+ with a fork at the end of the combination, giving Black a decisive material advantage. (0-1, 42)

David Howell vs. Jack Rudd: 39 Rg8+ forking the black king and bishop. 1-0

Richard Bates vs. Sarah Hegarty: 38 Nxg7! A knight sacrifice, tearing away part of Black's defensive wall and opening up the white rook to support an attack by the queen. 38 ... Kxg7 39 Qxh6+ Kf7 40 Qh7+ Kf8 41 Rxd7 1-0

Ameet Ghasi vs. Gyula Meszaros: 11 Qf3! Forking the knight on b7 and the pawn on f7. White will gain a significant material advantage. 11 ... Qd5 12 Qxf7+ Kd8 13 Qxg7 and 1-0 on move 17.

Peter Mercs vs. Thomas Thorp: 19 Qxe5! Exploiting the pin on the d-pawn. 19 ...dxe5 20 Rxd7 1-0

Gawain Jones vs. Donald Mason: 20 Bxg7! A sacrifice to blast a hole through the black king's defences. 20 ...Kxg7 21 Rg4+ Kh8 22 Qh6 1-0 If 27...Rg8 23 Qxh7+ Kxh7 24 Rh3+ mates.

Gawain Jones vs. Terry Chapman: 22 Bxe7+! Deflecting the black king from the defence of his rook. 22 ...Kxe7 If 22...Qxe7 23 Rb8+ wins. 23 Qxg8 1-0

Sarah Hegarty vs. Liam Varnam: 38 Ra4 checkmate. White takes advantage of the pinned b-pawn.

Dominic Mackle vs. Gawain Jones: 24 ...Ne2+ 0-1 If 25 Bxe2 Qxg2 checkmate, while 25 Kh1 and 25 Kh2 each allow 25 ...Qxh4 checkmate.

Alexander Longson vs. Richard Palliser: 39 ...Nd2+ A discovered check, which attacks a bishop at the same time. 40 Kh2 Nxc4 0-1 If 41 Rxc4 e2 and the pawn promotes to a queen.

Daniel Fernandez vs. Peter Wells: 29 ...Qxf3+! Winning a piece, due to 30 Kxf3 Nd2+, with a knight fork. (0-1, 33)

Charles Storey vs. Colin Purdon: 46 Rf4+! 1-0 The skewer wins the rook and, after the inevitable 47 Rxb4, White's rook is in the right place to stop the black b-pawn from queening.

David Eggleston vs. Sarah Hegarty: 59 Bxf6! 1-0 A pawn fork would follow after 59 ...Nxf6 60 e5+, when White would win the knight and be left with an easily winning king and pawn ending.

Jasper Tambini vs. Neil Carr: 35 ...Bxf4+! Deflecting the queen from its defence of the rook. 36 Qxf4 Qxc2 0-1

Solutions to 'Play Like Tal' positions

Mikhail Tal vs. Bob Wade: Tal wrapped it up with 40
Bxe6! Qxe6 41 Qg6+ and Bob Wade
resigned, 1-0. After the possible variation 41 ...Kh8, Tal
would force checkmate by 42 Rc7!

Mikhail Tal vs. Peter Kiriakov: Tal smashed through
Black's defence with 18 Rxe6! and Kiriakov resigned
immediately, 1-0. On 18 ...fxe6, 19 Qxg6+ destroys
the entire wall of pawns from around the black king,
leaving it in a hopeless position.

Mikhail Tal vs. Jan Timman: Tal is playing for
checkmate and he needs to get his knight to g5.
Timman is currently defending g5 with a pawn, so Tal
deflects it with a sacrifice. 18 Rxe5! fxe5 20 Ng5 Tal is
threatening 21 Bxg7 followed by 22 Qxh7 checkmate.
Timman prevents the main threat but his position
falls apart anyway. 20 ...Bf6 21 Nxe6 and Timman
resigned, 1-0.

Bibliography

Books

The Batsford Book of Chess by Bob Wade
(Batsford, 1991)

Chess Duels by Yasser Seirawan (Everyman
Chess, 2012)

Complete Games of Mikhail Tal (3 volumes) by
Hilary Thomas (Batsford, 1979-1980)

De la Bourdonnais versus McDonnell, 1834 by
Cary Utterberg (McFarland, 2005)

Fischer v. Spassky, Reykjavik 1972 by C.H.O'D
Alexander (Penguin, 1972)

Kasparov v Deeper Blue by Daniel King
(Batsford, 1997)

My Great Predecessors (series) by Garry
Kasparov (Everyman Chess, various dates)

Second Piatigorsky Cup by Isaac Kashdan
(Dover, 1968)

Taimanov's Selected Games by Mark Taimanov
(Everyman Chess, 1995)

*The Complete Games of World Champion
Anatoly Karpov* by Kevin O'Connell, David Levy
and Jimmy Adams (Batsford, 1976)

The Games of Tigran Petrosian, vols. 1 and 2 by
Eduard Shekhtman (Everyman Chess, 1991)

Software

ChessBase

Fritz

Websites

The Week in Chess

www.theweekinchess.com

ChessBase

chessbase.com

Index